Unto These Hills

A DRAMA OF THE CHEROKEE

By

KERMIT HUNTER

The University of North Carolina Press

Copyright, 1950, by
THE CHEROKEE HISTORICAL ASSOCIATION, Inc.
Cherokee, N. C.
Printed in the United States of America
THE STEPHENS PRESS, ASHEVILLE, N. C.

Foreword

THE ESTABLISHING of an outdoor drama in the Great Smokies involved years of work by a number of people in western North Carolina. Most of them were descendants of the Indians and whites who lived this story a hundred years ago and who at last saw their ancestors come to life on the stage of *Unto These Hills*. It was for these people that the play was written.

Every courtesy and assistance was given by Superintendent Joe Jennings and other officials of the Cherokee Indian Agency. Important advice and suggestions came from Chief Henry Bradley, Vice-Chief McKinley Ross, along with Meroney French, Moses Owle, George Owl, Anderson Saunooke, Arsene Thompson, Mrs. Emily Walkingstick, Mrs. Mollie Arneach, and other members of the Eastern Band of the Cherokee Nation. Valuable assistance and encouragement were given by Ross and Louise Caldwell, Mary Ullmer, Sam Gilliam, and the people of Cherokee. For much of the history and traditions of pioneer days the author drew upon information given by George M. Stephens, of Asheville, and Mrs. Sadie S. Patton, of Hendersonville.

Officials of the Cherokee Historical Association were understanding and cooperative at all times, especially Chairman Harry E. Buchanan, of Hendersonville, who supervised the entire production; Percy Ferebee, of Andrews; Kelly Bennett, of Bryson City; and others.

In addition, the author received sound technical advice from Paul Green, Josephina Niggli, and Walter Pritchard Eaton, of Chapel Hill, while a great deal of credit goes to Foster Fitz-Simons, Kai Jurgensen, Lynn Gault, and those members of the Carolina Playmakers' staff who gave time and attention to the drafting of the play.

Above all, the author is deeply indebted to Samuel Selden and Harry Davis, whose keen criticism and constant help were so vital. To Mr. Selden, who conceived and fostered the play, and to Mr. Davis, who so capably directed its first production, this book is respectfully dedicated.

KERMIT HUNTER

Chapel Hill
January 1951

Cast of Characters

NARRATOR
CHIEF of the Cherokee in 1540
KOTANGA, a Seminole guide
HERNANDO DE SOTO
TECUMSEH, chief of the Shawnee
WHITE PATH, war-chief of the Cherokee
JUNALUSKA
DROWNING BEAR
SEQUOYAH
WHITE MISSIONARY
LEWIS CASS, adjutant of Jackson's command
ANDREW JACKSON
SAM HOUSTON
DOCTOR
MRS. PERKINS, a pioneer woman
WILANI, wife of Tsali
TSALI, a Cherokee warrior
MONK, a prospector
BRAD TURNER, a frontiersman
STOREKEEPER
REVEREND JOHN F. SCHERMERHORN
MR. REED, his assistant
WILL THOMAS
ELIAS BOUDINOT, a Cherokee preacher
DANIEL WEBSTER
NUNDAYELI, daughter of Tsali
ANN WORCESTER
REVEREND SAM WORCESTER, a missionary
SUYETA, son of Drowning Bear
MAJOR DAVIS
LIEUTENANT

2

DRUNKEN SOLDIER
WILLIAM HENRY HARRISON
Indian villagers, white settlers, Spanish soldiers, U. S. soldiers, dancers, loiterers, etc.

TIME
The early part of the nineteenth century

PLACE
The Great Smokies; Washington, D. C.; Georgia; Alabama

ACT I
Scene 1: A Cherokee village, 1540
Scene 2: Council of chiefs, 1811
Scene 3: Horseshoe Bend, Alabama, March 27, 1814
Scene 4: A clearing in the woods, 1814
Scene 5: A country store New Echota, Georgia, 1835
Scene 6: Council of chiefs, 1835
Scene 7: A meadow near New Echota, Georgia, 1835
Scene 8: A room in the White House, 1836
Scene 9: A Cherokee village, 1838

ACT II
Scene 1: The village, 1838
Scene 2: Tsali's cave in the mountains, the following afternoon
Scene 3: The village, next morning
Scene 4: A room in the White House, 1841
Scene 5: The village, 1842

The characters and events of this play are drawn from actual historical records. Certain modifications have been made in the interest of dramatic unity.

All photographs in this book were taken by Vivienne Roberts, official photographer for *Unto These Hills*.

Act One

SCENE 1

(The play opens with a sustained prelude by a great chorus of mixed voices accompanied by the organ. The music is majestic, spirited, triumphant, expressing the vast, boundless freedom of the open world. The prelude gradually merges into a pastoral quietness as the voice of the Narrator is heard.)

NARRATOR

In the beginning was the land—plains and valleys of green grass—forests of rich oak, and poplar, and pine—tall mountains pushing their smooth ancient peaks against the sky.

In the beginning was freedom, the freedom of green things growing, of sun and wind and rain—the freedom of laughter—freedom of work, and play.

In the beginning was peace, the peace of common brotherhood, common worship, common labor. The land was friendly and bountiful.

(As the Narrator continues, a faint glow on the center stage reveals a throne-like seat up center and the fronts of Indian long houses of a bygone era. An Indian chief in feathered cape and headdress sits on the raised seat, and on either side is a dancer with his back to the audience, each on his knees and bent forward with his face against the ground. The dancers are dressed in loin cloths and moccasins.)

Far up, where velvet sunlight poured through the cool ravines of the Oconaluftee River, where soft winds made the yellow corn tassel blow through the lazy mid-summer, lived the Great Spirit—that divine force which stirred the hearts of all men, and which led them to express, in primitive ecstasy, their deep kinship with the eternal God.

(*The two figures have risen slowly to their knees, lifting their arms and gazing upward.*)

The black bear and the gray foxes know the earth is wide.
My brother the fox spoke and said,
"Now is the time of sun in the green corn;
Behold and see the wideness of the earth!
Stand by cool water and say to the white clouds:
You are my strength; the power is yours, O heavens!"

(*The two figures have now risen to their feet, heads back and arms still upraised. The music changes suddenly to a spirited Indian dance. Lights come up on the center stage. The two figures leap down center as a crowd of dancers pours onto the stage. The dance is sweeping and vivid, lasting for several minutes, finally leading to a tempestuous climax. As the dance closes, other villagers hurry onto the stage from both sides, laughing, talking, applauding. The music merges into a gay mood as the scene becomes one of laughter and movement, children playing, villagers running to and fro. As the stage fills with people, the Chief lifts his arms and gazes upward. The people respond by lifting their arms and facing the Chief. The leader lowers his arms slowly, claps his hands once, and again the villagers come to life. They hurry in and out bringing containers of food, ears of corn, baskets, handiwork, and various items to occupy themselves. The men are polishing and testing their spears, bows and arrows, blowguns. Children play, and the scene is one of substance and bounty. The Narrator continues.*)

In the beginning was the land. The Red Man possessed it lovingly. He possessed it with gentleness and humility, with peace.

(*The music changes to a tense, somber mood.*)

But out of the Great Sea to the east was destined to come a roaring wave which would destroy that peace—a seething tide of strange men with pale faces and restless hands. Up across the mountains it would burst and spread, a vast hungry tide of pioneers: seeking, grasping, building—fanning out in giant fingers across the plains, surging at last to the shores of the far west. And always before it, like dry leaves scattered in the winds of autumn, the Red Men would flee for their lives.

(The people, as if conscious of the words, undergo a subtle change, pausing in their activity, listening, gazing about into space. The gayety gradually subsides. They go on with their work, but they are slow and deliberate.)

White men would one day take the land in their hands and shake it. Hills and valleys would grow noisy with the clanking of hoe and spade, the ringing of ax and hammer, the crash of falling timber. The land would give forth its bounty to a fabulous race of white giants. Western plains would become a vast green lake of corn, a yellow ocean of wheat. The giants would build roads, churches, schools. They would chain lightning and thunder. They would take the land and shake it without mercy!

And a terrible price would be paid by the Red Man. Like a wild deer that trembles and steals away into the forests of time, he would halt in confusion, fall back, and turn furtively into the darkness of tragedy. And the most precious gift of humankind—the blessing of peace—would falter and die under the tramping feet of the white giants.

(The people are moving furtively toward the left, watching the Chief, who stands with arms folded. The lights diminish to a dim glow which falls across their faces as they merge into a frightened huddle at left.)

Always the strangers would come, more and more of them—pushing, yelling, sweating, cursing, blasting, hammering—men of oak and steel! And with them came fear—destruction—death!

(The music stops. The tense silence is suddenly broken by the sound of shots off right. The people, murmuring in fright and awe, gaze up the valley at

right where a dim glow illumines a pathway. There is another shot, then a man's agonized scream. From far right comes a youth, holding his side, staggering painfully toward the village. He reaches the stage, stumbles up center, and falls heavily on his face before the Chief. The Chief stoops down, turns him over on his back and examines him. Slowly he straightens with a grim look, then makes an angry sweep with his arm. Four warriors from the crowd pick up the youth, two on either side, and hurriedly carry him off at left while the villagers mourn pitifully. After a moment the four warriors hurry back in, muttering ominously. The men seize spears, bows, arrows, hatchets, and then they surge toward the right. The Chief suddenly waves them to halt, and they stand motionless. From the valley up right the silence is broken by the sound of men singing. The tune is a kind of marching song with indistinguishable words. As the people stand in awe, the singing comes nearer. A column of Spanish soldiers comes into view off right. Their song is an old folk lay sung idly and carelessly as they stride along in double file down the path. The light glistens on their breastplates, helmets, muskets, and lances. They make their way down to the stage, led by a gaudily-dressed Indian guide, along with their leader, De Soto, a bearded, arrogant Spaniard. The people shrink back to the left as the soldiers, also bearded and rough-looking, fill the stage right. De Soto surveys the villagers and the Chief a little scornfully. The Indian guide plants himself with an air of importance and slaps his chest as he speaks.)

GUIDE

My name is Kotanga!
   (*Pointing.*)
My people live south and east, many days journey, on the shore of the Great Sea.

(*The Chief surveys him, watches as the standard-bearer unfurls a flag and steps to the front, then he looks at the soldiers.*)

CHIEF

(*Pointing questioningly at the Spanish.*)
Who are these?

DE SOTO

(*With great dignity and arrogance.*)
Yo soy el capitán Hernando De Soto, criado de Su Majestad, rey de España! Estos son mis soldados!
(*The Chief stares, then looks toward the interpreter.*)

KOTANGA

His name is De Soto. He is a mighty warrior from a great king. Pale men came to our shores in many large canoes.
(*The Chief crosses, examines the banner, turns. Kotanga points to the banner.*)
Pale man says this land belongs to his king.
(*With an exclamation of anger, the Chief seizes the banner and flings it to the ground. The villagers and the soldiers leap to attention, as the warriors rush around down center with bows drawn and spears poised, and the Spanish level their muskets. Kotanga leaps between the two groups and frantically holds up his hands.*)

KOTANGA

Stop! You will bring death!
(*Indicating the Spanish.*)
They are called Askwani—my people say they come from the great god Wasi! Do what they say or they will kill you!
(*He slaps one of the breastplates.*)
Look! Nothing can harm them! They are spirits!
(*The people murmur in awe. The Chief waves his men back, then approaches the soldier and taps the breastplate curiously. At length he turns away and motions Kotanga to him. Meanwhile the people*)

gradually move nearer the Spanish and examine them in awe.)

CHIEF

Why is their skin white?

KOTANGA

Kotanga cannot tell. My people say they are moon gods. They kill men with the thunder stick. It pours out fire and smoke!

CHIEF

How can that be?

KOTANGA

It is true! Kotanga has seen it!
(*Pointing up the valley at right.*)
These are only a few. Over that mountain they are thicker than swarms of bees in the springtime!

CHIEF

(*Grimly.*)
What does the pale man want?

KOTANGA

(*Grandly.*)
The pale man looks for a land where arrows are tipped with pure gold—where men use turquoise for money—where children wear coral in their hair!

CHIEF

(*Impatiently.*)
Money? Cherokee do not understand money!
(*With a sweep of his arm.*)
The only gold we have is in the yellow cornfields!
(*Suddenly angry.*)
Tell the pale man to go!

KOTANGA

(*To De Soto.*)
El jefe dice que los hombres blancos tienen que salir!

DE SOTO

(*With a snarl.*)
Deseamos comida!

Kotanga

(*Turning.*)
White chief will stay! He wants food!
(*The Chief turns grimly toward the left and motions to the warriors. Four men enter carrying the dead youth. They lay him on the ground at the feet of the Chief, who turns to De Soto and indicates the body. The Spaniard glances down scornfully, then shrugs.*)

De Soto

Un muchacho no importa. Servimos el rey de España! Donde está el oro?

Kotanga

White chief wants gold!
(*The Chief whirls angrily, goes to the warriors and jerks from their necks several trinkets and strings of metal beads. He crosses to De Soto and flings them defiantly on the ground at his feet. There is a tense silence as De Soto kicks the trinkets disgustedly with his toe.*)

De Soto

Annh! Dos pepitos!
(*The Chief watches the Spaniard for a moment, then draws himself up and points toward the left.*)

Chief

Tell the pale man to go three moons' journey toward the setting sun. There he will find a land where rivers flow with gold and where arrows are tipped with silver!

Kotanga

(*To De Soto, pointing off left.*)
Nos vamos mas allá! Mucho oro!
(*Again De Soto snarls angrily, then finally he motions to his men and points toward the left.*)

De Soto

Hombres!—vámonos!
(*Resuming their marching song, the soldiers fall into formation and march quickly off left, led by*

Kotanga and De Soto. As the column moves out of sight, the song dies away in the distance. The lights diminish to a faint glow on the faces of the people as they gaze off left in awe. The organ comes up as the lights go down, and the voice of the Narrator is heard.)

SCENE 2

NARRATOR

Two hundred and fifty years roared by. The white men kept coming. Good met with good; evil with evil. The Cherokee tried to keep peace: like all people who live close to the earth, close to the sun and rain and the turning of the seasons, they had learned that no matter what a man's race or color might be, it is far better to live with him in friendliness, because hatred bites into the souls of men.

But now England was again threatening the new continent. Even the mountains to the south were swept with turmoil. And so it was that on a certain October morning in the year 1811, here in the valley of the Oconaluftee River, the Cherokee chieftains, from many days' journey, were called to solemn council by the mighty Junaluska, whose deep quiet words were like east wind in the forest. A certain warrior had come down from the north, out of the Shawnee nation, down through Kentucky and Tennessee, shouting in words of flame. Already his name had flashed through the country like chain lightning: The Shooting Star of the Shawnee, from distant Ohio—Tecumseh!

(During the narration a red glow of light on the stage at audience left reveals a clearing in the woods, a semicircle of chiefs around the area, and a stump down center. In a high place is Junaluska, and near him Sequoyah, Drowning Bear, John Ross, White Path, a white missionary, and several others.

Junaluska lifts his hand; the others respond, then all sit down. Tecumseh comes in quickly from the left, followed by two painted warriors who stand at left with arms folded. Tecumseh is a fiery, vigorous man, yet there is a cold kind of scorn in his manner. The war paint and typical Indian costumes of the Shawnee form a sharp contrast to the simple buckskin of the Cherokee. Tecumseh's headband carries a white and red feather above his forehead. He moves up center, raises his hand to Junaluska, who rises to respond and then sits down.)

TECUMSEH

(Indicating the feathers.)

Tecumseh wears two feathers. The white feather means brotherhood of all Indians. To the great chief, Junaluska, Tecumseh brings friendship.

(Palms outward.)

The mother of Tecumseh was a Cherokee. Shawnee and Cherokee are born to be brothers.

(Suddenly he strides down center as his voice hardens.)

The red feather means death to all white men! Shawnee are ready! What is the answer of the Cherokee?

(There is a tense silence.)

What is the answer of the Cherokee? Will no man speak?

(White Path, impetuous and loud-voiced, leaps to his feet.)

WHITE PATH

White Path is war chief of the Cherokee—White Path joins Tecumseh!

(A murmur runs through the assembly, then a clear, refined voice is heard.)

ROSS

Wait!

(As they grow silent.)

First let Tecumseh tell his plan.

(Tecumseh strides impatiently toward Ross, surveys him scornfully.)

TECUMSEH

Who is this white rabbit in the council of the Cherokee?

JUNALUSKA

(Rising quickly.)
John Ross, of Georgia! He is seven-eighths white, but he is Cherokee!

TECUMSEH

(Pointing toward the missionary.)
Who is that one?

JUNALUSKA

He is a missionary, a man of God. He comes here with Sequoyah. He is our brother.
(Crossing his arms.)
Let Tecumseh tell his plan.

TECUMSEH

(Suddenly driving his black tomahawk viciously into the stump.)
There is Tecumseh's plan!
(Striding about with sweeping gestures.)
From the northern lakes to the Gulf of Mexico we will join together in one great nation. Choctaw will sweep the coast from Florida to Mississippi. Creeks will burn the towns in Alabama and south Georgia. Cherokee will destroy the settlements in north Georgia, in Tennessee, in western North Carolina.
(Pointing ominously.)
From the Peaks of Otter in Virginia, to Catawba Town in South Carolina, the Cherokee will draw a line.
(A pause, then grimly.)
Never again will white men cross that line!
(There is a sharp silence as the chiefs look at each other.)

ROSS

Where will the Shawnee fight?

TECUMSEH
(*Quickly.*)
Two thousand Shawano are waiting in southern Indiana, at a place called Tippecanoe. The brother of Tecumseh is leading them.

ROSS
What if the Cherokee say no?

TECUMSEH
(*With a snarl of disgust.*)
White men from across the sea have come to help us. They will give back what is ours! If the Cherokee say no, Tecumseh and his people will join the British!
(*Several of the chiefs leap to their feet and talk excitedly to each other.*)

JUNALUSKA
(*Silencing the crowd.*)
Wait!
(*As they grow quiet.*)
Has Tecumseh tried to make peace with the white man?

TECUMSEH
Peace? Hah! The white man is like a hungry wolf—he *takes* what he wants!
(*Striding about, with increasing sarcasm.*)
The white man says, "Go see the Governor." The white governor of Indiana, William Henry Harrison, says, "Go see the President." The President sits far away in Washington and sips his wine. He says, "Go see Congress!" All the time our people are tricked and cheated out of everything they own!
(*Coldly.*)
Tecumseh talks no more.
(*With a sudden shout.*)
The time has come to fight!
(*Again the chiefs leap to their feet in a frenzy of excitement.*)

JUNALUSKA
Wait! Stop!

(Tecumseh, pressing his advantage, seizes one of his men, points out a hideous scar that runs from the man's throat around to his ear.)

TECUMSEH

Look at that scar! White men did that! White men must die!

WHITE PATH

White Path remembers the day his father was murdered by a drunken white man! He remembers the day his mother was trampled by a white man's horse! Here in the mountains you talk of peace, but in Georgia the Cherokee are treated like animals! We must kill!

(Many of the chiefs are shouting their approval.)

TECUMSEH

(Boldly triumphant.)

Who will be on the side of Tecumseh and drive out the white man?

(The chiefs are raising their arms and shouting. Junaluska calls angrily.)

JUNALUSKA

Stop! Stop! Wait! Stop!

(The chiefs hesitate.)

Sit down! You are Cherokee chiefs, not a flock of jaybirds!

(They sit down slowly, glancing first at Tecumseh, then at Junaluska.)

TECUMSEH

(Crossing his arms impatiently.)

The Cherokee have a constitution like the white man. Your constitution says that a majority will rule. You see how the chiefs have voted—what more do you want?

JUNALUSKA

(Grimly.)

Junaluska knows the constitution of the Cherokee better than Tecumseh does. In this council every man speaks. Let Tecumseh keep still for a while!

(Tecumseh turns away with a shrug of scorn.)
From the far south comes one who knows the history and wisdom of the white man. Already he is building a new language, so our people can print books, and read, and learn. This man is a Christian, like all of us.
(Firmly.)
First, the Cherokee will listen to Sequoyah.
(The chiefs glance toward Sequoyah as he rises slowly. He is a quiet man of forty, his voice calm and clear, and his manner commanding in spite of the fact that he uses a cane. His effect on the others is instantaneous. He glances around the circle of chiefs, then fixes on Tecumseh.)

SEQUOYAH
The people from the north have spoken the truth; they told us Tecumseh had the cunning of a panther. They said he was clever as the red fox. Now Sequoyah will ask three questions.
(There is a tense silence as Tecumseh turns slowly and faces Sequoyah.)
Does Tecumseh have guns?

TECUMSEH
We use the weapon of the Red Man!—bow and arrow, knife, tomahawk, fire!

DROWNING BEAR
(Leaping to his feet.)
Against the guns of the white man?

TECUMSEH
Are you afraid?
(The chiefs seem suspicious, however, as they mutter among themselves. Drowning Bear sits down slowly, watching Tecumseh.)

SEQUOYAH
Thirty years ago the British were driven out of this country. Now they come again. Suppose the Red Man joins

the British—suppose the British take back the land—does Tecumseh think they will give it to the Red Man?

TECUMSEH

(*Irritated.*)

The British have promised us all the land west of the mountains!

SEQUOYAH

Tecumseh himself said the white man was like a hungry wolf. The British are white!

(*Again the chiefs look at each other and mutter in low tones.*)

Now Sequoyah asks the third question: years ago we lived in caves and grass huts—today we build warm houses. Many times we used to starve through the long winter—now we plant big fields of corn and potatoes, and store food in barns for the winter. Our fathers prayed to the spirits of these mountains—now we go to church and worship a Christian God. *Where did the Red Man learn these things?*

TECUMSEH

Where did the Red Man learn to scalp his enemies? Where did he get smallpox?

(*To the chiefs quickly, as he points to Sequoyah.*)

You hear? Sequoyah is trying to trick his people!

SEQUOYAH

Tecumseh tells us to trust the British. He tells us to fight without guns. He says to go back and live the way our fathers did, like animals!

(*To the chiefs.*)

Stop and think! There is only one way to go! The white man is thicker than the leaves of these forests! If we fight, we will surely be destroyed!

TECUMSEH

(*Bitterly.*)

Is Sequoyah afraid?

SEQUOYAH
Yes.
TECUMSEH
Of the white man?
SEQUOYAH
No—of the Red Man.
TECUMSEH
(*To the others.*)
The clever Sequoyah speaks in riddles!
SEQUOYAH
The Red Man is simple and trusting. When he is hurt, he goes crazy and tries to hurt back. Where does it all end?
(*Grimly.*)
We must stop killing, stop hating, stop fighting!
TECUMSEH
(*Wildly vehement.*)
Stop fighting? And let the white buzzards pick our bones?
SEQUOYAH
We must call the American government to council and make a treaty.
TECUMSEH
(*With sarcasm.*)
What kind of a treaty?
SEQUOYAH
A treaty to live in peace!
TECUMSEH
With these white settlers? Hah!
(*To the chiefs.*)
Tecumseh offers you a treaty with the Shawnee, the Creeks, all the Red Men in this country!
WHITE PATH
Tecumseh is a strong man! Never before have the Shawnee asked to be our friends! Never have we had peace

with the Creeks. Now our homes are being taken away by the white man, and our people murdered!

(*Pointing to Sequoyah.*)

Everyone knows that man is a fool and a dreamer—why should the Cherokee listen to him?

SEQUOYAH

(*Grave and intense.*)

Many years ago, around the council fire, Sequoyah listened to the wise old chiefs. This is what they told me when I was a boy. They said: It is not that a man's skin is black, or red, or white. Some men are good—some men are evil! A good man never screams for revenge—he labors for peace! We are not Red Men! We are Americans!

TECUMSEH

(*Angry and scornful.*)

Americans—hah! You are cowards! Is that your answer?

SEQUOYAH

This is Sequoyah's answer!

(*Raising his right hand.*)

From this day forward he swears to live in peace with the white man! Who will join with Sequoyah?

(*There is a pause, then one by one the chiefs get to their feet, all except White Path. Tecumseh is in a rage. Sequoyah quickly comes down center, seizes the black tomahawk, and wrenches it out of the stump. He gazes at Tecumseh for an instant, then with a sudden sweep of his arm he flings the tomahawk viciously on the ground at Tecumseh's feet. One of Tecumseh's men grabs the tomahawk quickly and raises it, but Tecumseh waves him back. The Shawnee chief draws himself up, surveys the circle of chiefs, then suddenly whirls and runs off in the darkness at left, followed quickly by his two men. White Path sits down and buries his face in his hands.*)

SEQUOYAH

(*Gazing into space.*)

Above, Cherokee harvest festival in the sixteenth century. *Below,* The Chief (Cain Saunooke) examines the Spanish banner as De Soto (Eugene Graves) draws his sword.

Above, Kotanga (William Greene) explains to the Chief that the Spaniards seek gold. *Below,* De Soto leads his men westward in search of gold.

Above, Tecumseh (Blanton Miller) demands that the Cherokee join the Shawnee. *Below*, Houston (James Wood) and Cass (Robert Thomas) study a map at Horseshoe Bend.

Above, Andrew Jackson (Artus Moser) questions Creek prisoners. *Below,* The prisoners slip out of their bonds and look for an opportunity to kill Jackson.

In the west, beyond the Father of Waters, lie the Great Plains and the western mountains. Perhaps the Cherokee will have to go there some day.
>   (*Intensely.*)

Whether you go to the West or stay here, remember this: you have chosen the way of peace—you have taken the white man as your brother. Let no man forget this day!

SCENE 3

NARRATOR

To the north flamed the hatred of the Shawnee. To the south rose the scorn of the Creeks. But in the hour of decision the choice had been made.

With bitter self-denial and with strong determination, the Cherokee finally made their way into the confidence of the white men. Even though they received little kindness or respect, they followed their chiefs and held fast to the ideal of peace.

Suddenly the white men called on the Cherokee for help —help against these other Indians who threatened the American nation. Would the Cherokee take up arms against their own race? Would they help the white man preserve the very land he had taken from them? A strange thing to ask!

And yet—down from the high peaks and sunny foothills of the Great Smokies, from the broad valleys of Georgia and Tennessee, from cabins and pine-board huts, farms and villages, the Cherokee came—three thousand strong. For the first time since Revolutionary days the Cherokee fought side by side with white American soldiers.

>   (*Lights on the center stage reveal a clearing in the woods. There is the sound of firing off left, and the occasional roar of a cannon in the distance. Up left on a mound of rocks Junaluska peers off left watching the progress of the battle. Up right a doctor is treating several wounded men who are bandaged and bloody. One by one these men leave the stage during*

the scene. At a table up center sits Lewis Cass, the adjutant, studying a map. Beside him towers Sam Houston, a tall figure in buckskin, also gazing at the map.)

It was now shortly after daylight on the morning of March 27, 1814, in north Alabama, at a place called Horseshoe Bend. There was a clump of trees back of the Tallapoosa River, and in this spot, a hundred yards back of the front line, was the headquarters of General Andrew Jackson. Among Jackson's troops was a young white man from Tennessee, reared as a boy by the Cherokee. The Cherokee called him Kalanu, which means The Raven. His real name was Sam Houston.

(Houston crosses up left and stands with Junaluska peering off in the distance as Jackson strides in from the right. He stops to glance at the wounded men, then crosses hurriedly toward Houston and Junaluska.)

JACKSON

Sam, how does it look down there?

HOUSTON

Still the same, Andy.

JACKSON

Confound it! I thought that cannon would blast 'em out! Looks like cannon balls bounce off o' them logs like marbles! Might as well be usin' a slingshot!

(He reaches the mound and peers off left.)

JUNALUSKA

Let General Jackson be careful!

JACKSON

(Shouting to someone off left.)

Hey, Major! Send some men around on the west side! See if you can draw 'em out a little!

HOUSTON

Better get down off o' there 'fore you get killed!

(Jackson peers around once more, then he descends and crosses toward the table at center.)

JACKSON
(*Muttering angrily.*)
A thousand Creeks holed up in the bend o' that river, and we can't touch 'em! Cass, have you figured out that map yet?

CASS

Not yet, General.

JACKSON
(*Picking up the map and studying it.*)
How in tarnation can anybody read that mess o' chicken tracks! That's the army for you—send a man out in this stinkin' wilderness to fight a gang o' savages, and give 'im a puzzle to figure out!

HOUSTON

Get Junaluska to read it. He knows this country.

JACKSON
(*Turning to Junaluska as the Indian crosses toward the center.*)
All right—there it is.
(*Junaluska takes the map and glances at it, looks at Jackson, then turns the map right side up and looks at it again, shaking his head.*)

JUNALUSKA

No good.

JACKSON

Well, see if you can draw it right.
(*Junaluska goes to the table and takes a pencil to work on the map. Jackson turns and limps toward the mound up left.*)

HOUSTON

What are you limpin' for?

JACKSON

I got a danged nail in my boot!

HOUSTON

Well, here—take it off and lemme fix it.

(*Jackson sits at the foot of the mound. Houston draws off the boot and goes to work on it with his hunting knife. From the left Drowning Bear hurries in, followed by Tsali, who is shoving two prisoners with their hands tied. The prisoners, hideously painted, are surly and unmanageable.*)

JACKSON

What's all this?

DROWNING BEAR

General Jackson said bring some prisoners.

JACKSON

Where'd you get 'em?

DROWNING BEAR

Across the river.

JACKSON

(*Sharply.*)
What?

DROWNING BEAR

(*Nodding toward Houston.*)
Kalanu sent us.

JACKSON

(*To Houston.*)
Oh, you did, eh!
(*Rising quickly, turning to Drowning Bear.*)
You had orders to stay on this side! Who are you anyway?

DROWNING BEAR

I am Drowning Bear. This is my friend, Tsali.

TSALI

(*Proudly.*)
Tsali brought back two prisoners!

DROWNING BEAR

Drowning Bear brought back twenty-five canoes!
(*A soldier takes over the prisoners from Tsali.*)

JACKSON

(*Impatiently.*)
Canoes? What For?

DROWNING BEAR

Cherokee took the canoes and went down the river to cross. Now we burn the fort from behind.

JACKSON

(*Angrily.*)

From behind! Why, dang it, there's nothing back o' that fort but swamps! You go back down there and tell that gang o' Cherokee to stay where I put 'em! If General Coffee can't handle 'em, I'll send somebody that can! I want you to hold *the east bank o' that river*—is that clear?

DROWNING BEAR

(*Defiantly.*)

Too late! Cherokee crossed the river a long time ago!

JACKSON

(*In a rage.*)

Confound it, who's in command here—you or me?
(*Houston comes to the center quickly. Junaluska crosses to Jackson.*)

JUNALUSKA

Wait! Junaluska asked for volunteers to help General Jackson fight the British. Three thousand men came all the way to Alabama. Drowning Bear is in command!
(*Folding his arms grimly.*)
Is General Jackson ready to support the Cherokee?

JACKSON

While I'm in command, you'll take orders from me!
(*Drowning Bear and Junaluska turn away quickly. Houston puts his hand on Jackson's shoulder and mutters something quietly to him. Jackson looks at the two Indians, then at Houston, and finally yields.*)
All right! Go on! Go on, dang it! If you get through that swamp, we'll cut loose on this end!
(*Drowning Bear motions to Tsali, and they go out quickly at left. Jackson steps toward the two prisoners and surveys them, then turns to Junaluska.*)
Can these critters understand American?

JUNALUSKA

Yes.

JACKSON

(*To the prisoners threateningly.*)
How many Indians in that fort?
(*The prisoners look away in silence.*)
Any British over there? Any white men?
(*The prisoners refuse to answer.*)
Answer me, you dang stinkin' savages!
(*One of the prisoners whirls and spits in Jackson's face. Jackson raises his hand to strike the man.*)
Why, you—!

HOUSTON

(*Peering off left.*)
Wait—here comes a runner!
(*A young Indian rushes in from down left, hurries to Junaluska and mutters something, then turns and runs out again at left.*)

JACKSON

What is it?

JUNALUSKA

Cherokee are attacking the fort!

HOUSTON

(*Still peering.*)
Look! The whole place is on fire!
(*Jackson hurries to the mound, takes one look, then shouts to someone off left.*)

JACKSON

Hey, Major! Attack! Tell 'em to charge! Let that company on the west hold their position—put the rest in front!
(*Off left the firing increases, and there are shouts of "Charge!" Jackson turns to the others.*)
You men get down there and help! Run, Sam! You too, Cass!
(*The others hurry out at left, leaving Junaluska at*

the mound and the two prisoners down left. Jackson limps back toward the mound.)

Where's my boot, confound it!

(*At this moment the prisoners get their hands loose. One of them runs up center, apparently looking in the bushes for a weapon. The other steals along the foot of the mound toward Jackson. Junaluska turns and sees him.*)

JUNALUSKA

Look out!

(*He dives at the man, struggles with him, finally stabs him with his knife. The second prisoner starts across with a rock in his hand. Junaluska dives between him and Jackson, struggles with the man for a moment, finally stabs him. The man falls heavily. Junaluska straightens and gazes down at the body. Jackson comes slowly toward the center and puts out his hand. Junaluska slowly takes his hand, and the two men gaze at each other as the lights go down. The music rises, and the voice of the Narrator is heard.*)

SCENE 4

NARRATOR

Horseshoe Bend—one of the great victories of the War of 1812. A short time later at New Orleans, England's last grip on America was broken, and there was peace. But news traveled slowly in the American wilderness of 1814. The people here in the Great Smokies were still waiting to learn what had happened to their young men who had gone away two months before to fight for General Jackson.

(*The lights, coming up on the stage at audience left, reveal a clearing in the woods. On a boulder up center sits Wilani, a young Indian woman, weaving a basket that has a leather strap for the shoulder, a kind of hunting basket. At her foot is a small cradle which she rocks with her foot as she hums to herself and peers off into the distance. As the Narrator finishes, Mrs. Perkins enters from the right, a lusty pioneer woman. The music stops.)*

MRS. PERKINS

Wilani! Here you are!

WILANI

Hello, Mrs. Perkins!

MRS. PERKINS

My goodness, are you going to spend the rest of your life out here in the woods?

WILANI

(Glancing around with a smile.)
I wish I could, it's so beautiful! The April leaves are so tiny and green—so many birds and flowers. I've been trying to weave them all into this hunting basket. Do you think Tsali will like it?

MRS. PERKINS

Of course! Let me see—why, it's beautiful, Wilani! Now why can't I make baskets like that! Tsali will love it.

WILANI

(Anxiously.)
Do you think Tsali will come back?

MRS. PERKINS

(Sitting down.)
Don't talk like that. Of course he'll come back.

WILANI

Tsali is so foolish. He never takes care of himself. If General Jackson would let him, Tsali would fight the Creeks all by himself.

MRS. PERKINS

He'll be all right. Wilani, the first thing a young wife has to learn is not to worry about her stupid husband. Look at me—do you think I lose any sleep over George Perkins?

WILANI

But he didn't go to fight the Creeks.

MRS. PERKINS

He might just as well—he spends all his time in that cornfield! George Perkins had no business marryin' me—he should've married an ear o' corn!

(*Turning to the cradle and peering down fondly.*)

How's the baby? Oh, look—she's asleep! Isn't she beautiful! Nundayeli's going to be a real princess.

WILANI

Tsali wants many sons.

MRS. PERKINS

They all do. So does George Perkins. Like I tell 'im—if he wouldn't spend so much time in that cornfield—

(*Turning to Wilani.*)

Don't worry about Tsali. He'll be back, and he'll buy you that pretty red and yellow dress you've always wanted. Any day now they'll all come marchin' back, proud as roosters.

(*Wilani suddenly leaps to her feet and peers off right.*)

WILANI

Tsali!

(*Tsali hurries in, sets down his rifle and pack as Wilani rushes to meet him. They embrace fondly.*)

MRS. PERKINS

See! What did I tell you! Welcome home, Tsali! Did you win the battle?

TSALI

Cherokee always win!

MRS. PERKINS

Good! Were many of our Cherokee boys killed?

TSALI

The oldest son of Drowning Bear—he will not come back.

MRS. PERKINS
(Turning quietly toward the left.)
I guess I better go speak to Drowning Bear.
(As she goes out at left, Wilani leads Tsali to the cradle and he gazes down with a smile. She picks up the hunting basket, holds it out proudly to him as he smiles fondly at her. She helps him put it over his shoulder, then they embrace once more as the lights go down and the music rises. The voice of the Narrator is heard.)

NARRATOR
Through the Cherokee nation swept a wave of rejoicing. Indians and whites gathered in village after village to celebrate the great victory. And in the Great Smokies, Drowning Bear's village reached far into the primitive past and brought back a dance of triumph, so that their white friends might see it—the great Eagle Dance.
(The music changes to a steady, low, dance movement. A dim band of colored light across the center stage reveals a group of dancers in loin cloths, kneebells, and colorful eagle feathers. The dance moves to a brilliant climax as the lights finally go down once more and the music changes to a more sombre mood for the Narrator.)

SCENE 5

NARRATOR
But as the years marched by, the hopes of the Cherokee were slowly crushed by the rising tide of white settlers who shoved their way into the wilderness, grabbing land, building towns, taking what they wanted. The Indians were hurt and angry. Their honest efforts to be friendly and peaceable seemed to be met more and more with greed and corruption—and with hatred.
Then suddenly a storm came over the land. Three hundred years before, Hernando De Soto had been the first to cry "Gold!" and now 1835 found the Cherokee over-

run by white men seeking that same precious yellow metal. The frontier towns of north Georgia exploded with tumult and with terror.

(The lights come up on the small stage at audience right, showing the interior of a country store and saloon. There is a rude bar and counter up center, a table down left where three rough-looking frontiersmen, half drunk, are talking in loud voices. Back of the counter is the storekeeper, a large, substantial man, polishing glasses and rubbing the counter. The door at left bursts open and a flashily-dressed individual hurries in.)

MONK

All right, step up, everybody! I'm buyin' for the house! Come on, you polecats, wash the dust out o' your gullets! Here, George, fill 'em up!

(The men scramble to the bar, excited and eager.)

VOICE

North Georgia Minin' Company must o' declared a divvy-dend!

ANOTHER

(As they all laugh.)
You ain't sick are you, Monk?

MONK

Here, get a drink, everybody!
(They crowd around as Monk ceremoniously lifts his drink.)
Well, here's to the new mines.
(He downs his drink as the others stand in awe.)

VOICES

New mines?
Where?
Hey! What's that? New mines?
(Monk smiles and pulls out a handkerchief, unfolds it, shows them a large gold nugget.)
Look at that nugget!
Here, lemme hold it!

STOREKEEPER
(*A heavy, commanding voice.*)
Where'd you git it?

MONK
West Fork of the Chestatee River.
(*The men make a break for the door.*)
Hey, wait a minute! Ain't gonna do you no good to put in claims! I got every foot o' that land sewed up tight for the North Georgia Minin' Company. What we ain't got, the Indians can have!
(*The others groan with disappointment and saunter back to the table. Monk comes toward them glass in hand.*)

MONK
Yep, soon as I found out for sure, I rode in here and filed claim on purty nigh the whole county. Had to get old Bill Yancey out o' bed to lemme in his office. Yessiree—sewed up tight!

STOREKEEPER
When you gonna start workin' it?

MONK
Soon as we can move our equipment over from the East Fork.

STOREKEEPER
What're you plannin' to do about the Cherokee?

MONK
Cherokee?
(*A shrug.*)
Ain't plannin' to do nothin'!
(*The others laugh.*)

STOREKEEPER
Cherokee own every foot o' that land. They been there more'n a thousand years.
(*Monk sets down his glass, wipes his mouth, turns to go.*)

Monk

I reckon there's more'n one way o' dealin' with Indians!

(The others nod and mutter their approval as Monk hurries out. A moment later the door opens again and an Indian lad of nine or ten comes timidly inside, watches the men at the table.)

Storekeeper

Well, Tsawasi, what can I do for you? Come on in. It's all right.

(The boy hesitates, comes shyly across to the right.)
Come on over here and tell me what you want.
(Leaning over.)
Ay, that's it. Well, he's gettin' to be a big boy! His mother even sends him to the store by himself. What can I do for you, Tsawasi?
(The boy hands him a note.)
A note, huh? Ay, now lemme see—
(Opening the note ceremoniously, with mock seriousness.)
—pound o' loaf sugar, yeah—bag o' roasted coffee, yeah—three yards o' calico cloth, yep—hmm—all right, fix 'em up for you right now.

(He turns to the shelves. The door at left bursts open and two more rough-looking frontiersmen come in. One of them steps to the counter and slaps it with his hand.)

Brad

Give us a drink.

Storekeeper

Just a minute.

Brad

(Beating on the counter.)
I said give us a drink!

Storekeeper

(Firmly.)
I'm busy waitin' on a customer! Slow down a minute—I'll get to you!

(*The man glances at the Indian boy, who is watching him in awe.*)

BRAD

Is this what you're waitin' on?
(*He kicks at the boy.*)
Get outa here, you—
(*The boy dodges and moves around the counter at right.*)

STOREKEEPER

(*Coming out from behind the counter.*)
Leave that boy alone!

BRAD

(*Starting for the boy.*)
I'll teach 'im to stand there gawkin' at a white man—

STOREKEEPER

(*Shoving Brad backward.*)
I told you to leave that boy alone!

BRAD

(*Angrily.*)
Now look out, George!

STOREKEEPER

I said leave him alone!

BRAD

You're always takin' up for these redskins! Maybe you're part Indian yourself!

STOREKEEPER

(*Snapping his suspenders gingerly.*)
If I was, I'd be proud of it! These Cherokee 'bout the only decent citizens we got left around here! Least they get out and work their farms and tend to their own business. That's more'n I can say for a lot o' white trash I know! You touch that boy an' I'll skin you alive! Now get outa here!
(*The second man tries to pull Brad toward the door.*)

BRAD

One o' these days you'll wish you hadn't been so all-fired sweet on these stinkin' Indians!

STOREKEEPER
The only thing that stinks around here is you! Now get out!
BRAD
Aw, give us a drink, George!
STOREKEEPER
I said get out!
(*Brad spits on the floor angrily as the other man drags him to the door.*)
BRAD
You think just 'cause your old man fought at Yorktown—
(*The Storekeeper grabs a bottle from the table and is about to fling it at Brad as the two men go out quickly. One of the drunks hurries to the Storekeeper and retrieves the bottle, staggering backward toward the counter and nursing the bottle lovingly. The Storekeeper shoves him back toward the table and goes angrily behind the counter. The door bursts open again and Schermerhorn strides in, a tall man dressed in black. He is followed by Reed, dressed the same.*)
SCHERMERHORN
Howdy, everybody, howdy, howdy! Schermerhorn's the name—the Reverend John F. Schermerhorn. Howdy, Mr. Bartender!
(*The Storekeeper nods.*)
My friend, Mr. Reed, and I were just passing through—thought we'd sorta drop in and get acquainted!
STOREKEEPER
Where you from?
SCHERMERHORN
Washington—Washington, D. C. Down here on government business.
STOREKEEPER
Well, step up an' have a drink.
(*Pouring.*)

Oh—excuse me—reckon you don't want none, seein' you're a preacher.

SCHERMERHORN

Well, er—the fact is—

(*Glancing toward the bottle.*)

—seein' as we're here on government business—ain't doin' any preachin' right now, you understand—

(*Clearing his throat.*)

—guess I will have a little something for my cough.

STOREKEEPER

(*Filling two glasses.*)

What kind o' business brings you down here from Washington?

SCHERMERHORN

(*Picking up his glass.*)

Figgerin' on makin' kind of a deal with the Indians.

(*He downs his drink, wipes his mouth.*)

Government's decided they might offer to buy this land from the Cherokee.

VOICES

Buy it?

SCHERMERHORN

Ay, that's Andy Jackson for you! Greatest president we ever had! I tell you, brothers, he's got the interest of the people at heart—the common people, yes sir!

STOREKEEPER

The government wants to buy this land? What for?

SCHERMERHORN

Make all this country government land—sell it for homesteads, so more white people can move in here. Yep! Gonna have a meeting up at Red Clay, Tennessee, next week. Soon as we can buy this land, we'll move the Indians out west, make room for more white people.

(*The group begins whispering in excitement.*)

Pass the word around. We want all the Indians to attend that meeting. Guess we better be going, Mr. Reed. Yep, it'll be a great day!

Above, Wilani (Eileen Smith) and Mrs. Perkins (Irene Bewley). *Below*, Mrs. Perkins questions Tsali (John Shearin) on the Battle of Horseshoe Bend.

Above, Charles Morrell, principal dancer, leads the famous Eagle Dance. *Below,* The triumphant Eagle Dance following the victory at Horseshoe Bend.

Above, The Storekeeper (Ralph Smith) asks Monk (D. C. Huntley) about the discovery of gold. *Below,* Schermerhorn (Peter Strader) announces the New Echota meeting.

Above, Schermerhorn calls on the people to sign the agreement. *Below,* The Cherokee minister, Boudinot, (Arsene Thompson) urges his people to accept the offer.

STOREKEEPER

A great day for who?

SCHERMERHORN
(*Turning in the doorway.*)

Yep, thanks to Andy Jackson, I reckon this'll be about the best thing that ever happened to the Cherokee!

(*The lights go down and the music rises momentarily.*)

SCENE 6

(*The lights come up on the small stage at audience left, showing the same semicircle of chiefs in the woodland clearing. White Path, hardly able to control himself, paces back and forth down center.*)

WHITE PATH

Junaluska tells us to be friendly! The Cherokee try to make friends, and the white man spits in his face! Now the Cherokee must fight!

JUNALUSKA

The white man has offered us a treaty!

WHITE PATH

Treaty? Hah! Fifty cents an acre for everything we own! Not one penny for our houses, our barns, our livestock, our fences—fifty cents an acre! Does Junaluska have a deed for his property? No—he is not an American citizen—maybe you'll not get anything! The same for all of us!

(*Clenching his fists.*)

The Cherokee run away like cowards. Tecumseh said twenty years ago to fight. Here we sit, listening to John Ross and Junaluska, talking about Sequoyah, and the white man comes over us like fire in the mountain! Well —what do you say now? What does Drowning Bear say?

DROWNING BEAR
(*Rising slowly.*)

Twenty years now the Cherokee have moved into the hills, up the narrow valleys, more and more into the high mountains. Our good farm lands are gone. We have nothing but scrubby hillsides!

(*Sinking to his seat helplessly.*)
Drowning Bear does not know what to say!

WHITE PATH

What about Junaluska?

JUNALUSKA

(*With feeling.*)
When Junaluska sees old men and women, children, and sick people, driven out like animals, he remembers what Sequoyah said: Someday all of us may have to go to the West.

(*Palms outward.*)
But now the white man says he will *buy* the land, and give the Cherokee money in return! What else can the Cherokee do?

ROSS

(*Rising quickly.*)
We can refuse to sell! If the white man wants a treaty, let him offer a good treaty! We will not sell unless we get a fair price!

WHITE PATH

(*Scornfully.*)
Does the Principal Chief think the Cherokee will ever get a fair price?

ROSS

We have friends in Washington! All of us fought with Jackson at Horseshoe Bend. Daniel Webster is our friend —he sent us a letter—here!

(*He draws out an envelope and hands it to White Path, who turns away in anger.*)

WHITE PATH

Our people die like dogs, and the Principal Chief gets a letter! Always the Cherokee run from the white man!

Even Drowning Bear brings a white man into the council of the Cherokee!

(*Drowning Bear leaps angrily to his feet.*)

JUNALUSKA

(*Pointing to the white man sitting beside Drowning Bear.*)

This is Drowning Bear's white son, Will Thomas. The eldest son of Drowning Bear died at Horseshoe Bend! White Path knows that Drowning Bear himself would die, if it would help the Cherokee—and so would Will Thomas. But do not ask a rabbit to fight a mountain lion!

WHITE PATH

(*In a rage.*)

My land is mine! It came to me from my fathers! Year after year I use it well—I never scar the soft earth with a plow—I tend it with my hands. It is all I have—White Path cannot live without his land!

ROSS

Listen to what I say—the white man wants to make a treaty—he is calling another meeting in December at New Echota. Tell the people they must not go to that meeting. The Cherokee will not give away their land for nothing!

WHITE PATH

(*Wildly.*)

Always the same words!—"wait, sit, do nothing"—you talk like a flock of women! The spirits of our fathers laugh at cowards! White Path is not a coward! He and his sons will die fighting like Cherokee!

ROSS

(*Grimly.*)

Twenty years ago the Cherokee took an oath to live in peace with the white man! Whoever breaks that pledge is a coward!

WHITE PATH

Then call White Path a coward! Let the peace chiefs run

up the narrow valleys into the high mountains! Let them fly to the west like groundhogs! White Path will fight! His people in Georgia will fight!

Junaluska

Wait!

(Stepping down center.)

Junaluska will go to Washington and talk to the President.

Drowning Bear

(Rising quickly.)

To Washington?

Junaluska

President Jackson is our friend—we fought side by side at Horseshoe Bend. Let White Path wait and keep peace!

(White Path turns away angrily and sits down.)

John Ross is the Principal Chief—let him go with Junaluska—to see the President!

(The lights go down quickly and the music rises.)

SCENE 7

Narrator

About this same time the famous composer of "Home Sweet Home," John Howard Payne, came to Tennessee to visit his friend, John Ross. Suddenly they were arrested in Tennessee by Georgia Guards, who came illegally across the line and took both men on a trumped-up charge. They were released after a short time, but it was too late. The government agents were moving fast—John Schermerhorn had been told to get some kind of a treaty signed and returned to the War Department. It was now December 29, 1835.

(As the music stops, the lights come up on the center stage, again a woodland scene. Benches and rude stools have been placed downstage, and toward the right is a platform with a table and chair. Schermerhorn and Reed are meeting and shaking hands with the Cherokee as they arrive.)

SCHERMERHORN
Now, let's make ourselves at home, brethern! Let's all get comfortable. Find a good place, everybody.
(*Coming downstage to meet an old woman.*)
Here's a place for you—that's right.
(*Nodding to others.*)
Good morning, brother! Good morning, sister! Mr. Reed, find a place for all our good friends here!
(*The man moves quickly, smiling and helping.*)
Everybody get a good seat—
(*He stops and peers off left, then suddenly his manner changes as he becomes lofty and pious.*)
The Lord bless you—find a place in the circle of the Lord—
(*Moving across toward the left as Elias Boudinot enters.*)
Well, well, well! Brother Boudinot!* Brother Elias Boudinot!
(*Hurrying to him with hand extended.*)
Glad to see you again, Elias! Come right up front here with me. Yep, always glad to meet another minister of the gospel. Lord bless us!
(*Leading Boudinot across toward the table.*)
Yes, sir! When Elias Boudinot's in favor of a thing, you can make up your mind it's all right.
(*Raising his hand in benediction.*)
Yes sir, the hand of the Lord is working today! He knows what is best for his people. Not a sparrow falls from its nest but what he sees and cares for it. Mr. Reed, watch them papers about to blow off the table. Yes sir, this is one of the great days of Cherokee history. Reverend Boudinot, I want you to sit up front here with me. Mr. Reed, bring a stool for Reverend Boudinot. Put it there.
(*Reed places a stool on the platform beside the table. Boudinot climbs up and sits down.*)
Now before we open this meeting, let's ask the Lord to be with us.

*The Cherokee used the English pronunciation, Boo-din-NOT.

(*He takes off his hat, lifts his arms, prays in a sing-song voice.*)

Lord, we want your blessing on these people here today. Bless the Cherokee nation and bring joy to the people. Make them good Christians and good citizens. Bless Elias Boudinot for his great work among his people, especially for writing all them good things in his newspaper this fall. He's got the faith, Lord, and that's something. Help him to guide his people the right way in this meeting. And bless Andrew Jackson. Amen.

(*Putting on his hat quickly.*)

Before we go any farther I want you to know that I represent the United States government. Last October, up at Red Clay, Tennessee, some of your chiefs didn't think so. You can all examine these papers any time you like.

(*Thumbs in his vest.*)

Now you all know why we're here. The Great White Father in Washington wants his children to have a good home, a place where they can hunt and fish and grow crops.

(*Sweeping gestures.*)

The President of the United States is giving you a great tract of land out beyond the Mississippi. He's giving you a new home, a place where game is plentiful, where the weather is good, and where each man can have all the land he wants. Andy Jackson is giving you this land free, my friends, absolutely free! and he's giving you five million dollars—just think of it—*five million dollars!*

(*The people murmur excitedly.*)

I tell you, Brother Boudinot, it's the hand of the Lord! It surely is the will of God!

(*Boudinot seems thoughtful. At this moment Drowning Bear enters from the right, followed by Tsali and Will Thomas. Thomas carries a mountain rifle. Schermerhorn glances at them, then again his manner changes; he becomes hurried and commanding as he addresses the crowd.*)

Now if there's no question, we'll go down to the ball

ground there by the river. All we have to do is take a vote, then I want each of you to sign the treaty. You can write your names right under the signature of President Andrew Jackson. Course, I don't have to tell you about Old Hickory, God bless 'im! He's the man that made all this possible. Now if there's no question, let's all go down to the river and have our picnic —
(*He is pointing toward the left and walking across, motioning the people to follow.*)

DROWNING BEAR
I have a question!
(*Schermerhorn stops, and the people wait anxiously.*)
I want to know what the treaty says.

SCHERMERHORN
If you don't mind, we'll take that up later. You see, all we're doing here today is getting the treaty signed. Anyway, it's about time for dinner. Now as I was saying—

DROWNING BEAR
Is the government agent trying to fool the people?

SCHERMERHORN
(*Coming back grimly.*)
Maybe you better identify yourself, brother!

DROWNING BEAR
I am Chief Drowning Bear. I own property in the Cherokee territory. This is my friend, Tsali, and my adopted son, Will Thomas.
(*Reed starts menacingly toward them.*)

SCHERMERHORN
Wait, Mr. Reed. Well, we're glad to have you, Mr. Drowning Bear! Make yourself at home! Now let's all get ready for dinner—
(*He starts away again.*)

DROWNING BEAR
(*Loudly.*)
What does the treaty say?

SCHERMERHORN
(Coming back to the table with a shrug toward the crowd.)

Very well, I guess we'll have to waste some more time. I'm gettin' hungry, ain't you?

(The people giggle. Schermerhorn picks up some of the papers, clears his throat.)

Now the treaty says the government will pay five million dollars for all this poor mountain land—five million dollars! The Cherokee get a big tract of land in the Indian territory where the western Cherokee now live, plus a big reserve in the Kansas Territory, all absolutely free! Besides that, the government will move the people, pay the bill, feed everybody on the way, and buy food and clothing for everybody for a whole year after they get there!

DROWNING BEAR
Who gets the money?

SCHERMERHORN
The General Council of the Cherokee Nation, I reckon.

DROWNING BEAR
Who's here to speak for the General Council?

SCHERMERHORN
We don't need anybody. When the treaty's ratified by Congress, the money'll be paid direct to the General Council.

(To the people with a laugh.)

You got to trust the U. S. government!

DROWNING BEAR
Where are the rest of the chiefs? Where's the Principal Chief, John Ross?

SCHERMERHORN
I don't know. Now we're wasting time—

TSALI
I'll tell you where he is! John Ross was arrested in Ten-

nessee by Georgia Guards and taken to jail so he couldn't come to this meeting.
(*Pointing at Schermerhorn.*)
You're afraid of him!

SCHERMERHORN
I don't know anything about that!

THOMAS
Mr. Schermerhorn, how does the government propose to move the people?—In wagons? Horseback? On Foot?

SCHERMERHORN
(*Defensively.*)
That hasn't been decided yet.
(*To the people.*)
You can trust Andy Jackson!

TSALI
Our people have a right to know! How will the money be divided? How much for an acre of land? How much for a house, a barn, a cow? How much for a mile of rail fence?

SCHERMERHORN
That'll be decided later.
(*Starting off at left.*)
Now if everybody will follow me down to the picnic—
(*The people are rising and moving toward the left. Drowning Bear leaps up onto the platform excitedly.*)

DROWNING BEAR
Listen, everybody! You are my people! Listen to the truth! The General Council voted against this treaty! These men are trying to trick you! Go home, before you get robbed!

TSALI
Go home, everybody—let the chiefs take care of this!
(*The people hesitate, murmuring in confusion.*)

SCHERMERHORN
Wait!
(*Striding slowly back toward the platform.*)

Now we appreciate the kind advice of Mr. Drowning Bear and—what's his name—Tsali—and we're proud to have these great men here; but this is something for you to decide for yourselves! You're the Cherokee people! This is a free country!

(*In a low grim tone.*)

You know something: the chiefs are too stubborn to attend this meeting. The chiefs are rich—you know that! They own lots of land—they keep Negro slaves—they're just trying to save their own hides, while you have to suffer!

DROWNING BEAR

That's a lie!

SCHERMERHORN

Very well! Let's ask Elias Boudinot!

(*Boudinot sits with his head bowed.*)

There he sits, a full-blooded Cherokee. For years he's watched over you. He founded your newspaper—he built the schools at New Echota and Spring Place. He's not rich, like some of your chiefs. He's a poor man, a minister of the gospel, like me! We're simple men—we don't know how to deliver fine speeches and make a lot of money! All we want to do is bring peace and joy to the people. Listen to Elias Boudinot—come on, Elias—speak to your people. It's your sacred duty, Elias!

(*With great humility, and with a worried glance at Drowning Bear and Tsali, Boudinot rises, speaks with simplicity and deep feeling.*)

BOUDINOT

What can I say? I am a poor Cherokee. My life is devoted to my people. Perhaps it would be better to move to some new country—

DROWNING BEAR

Elias!

BOUDINOT

We need churches, schools, hospitals. Can a handful of Cherokee fight the State of Georgia and the United States government?

                    DROWNING BEAR
Elias! Stop!
                    BOUDINOT
As God is my witness, I want to do what is right. Why
not accept this kind offer? We have fought long enough
—let us seek peace!
> (*The people nod in approval. Schermerhorn grabs
> Boudinot's hand and starts off toward the left.*)

                    SCHERMERHORN
Fine speech, Elias! That settles it—praise the Lord! Now
let's all go down to the picnic ground. We'll sign the
treaty and get our five million dollars.
                    DROWNING BEAR
> (*Shouting after the people.*)

No! Junaluska is going to Washington to see the President! He will help us!
                    SCHERMERHORN
> (*Urging the stragglers.*)

That's right. Go down to the picnic grounds. Enjoy yourselves!
> (*The people leave, all except Boudinot. Schermerhorn gazes after them, turns and struts toward the center, then stops and glances scornfully at Drowning Bear.*)

Hah!
> (*Raising his hand after the departed people.*)

Praise the Lord!
> (*Drowning Bear, unable to control his rage, seizes Schermerhorn by the neck, whirls him around and begins to strangle him. Schermerhorn struggles helplessly, calling hoarsely for his assistant. Reed grabs Drowning Bear and pulls him off, then is about to throw him down.*)

                    THOMAS
> (*Leveling his rifle.*)

Let him go!

(*Reed releases Drowning Bear as Schermerhorn recovers himself, sputters and coughs.*)

SCHERMERHORN
(*Hoarse with anger.*)
I represent the United States government! I'll have you arrested for this!

THOMAS
Let's see you try to arrest him!

SCHERMERHORN
(*Eyeing the rifle and pulling himself together.*)
All right, Mr. Drowning Bear. I'm willing to forgive and forget—let bygones be bygones. Here's my hand.
(*Drowning Bear turns away, ignoring the proffered handshake.*)
You gentlemen stay and have dinner with us.

DROWNING BEAR
Drowning Bear does not eat with buzzards!

TSALI
Elias, our people will call you a traitor!

BOUDINOT
(*Earnestly.*)
I did what I thought was right! We must have peace!

DROWNING BEAR
Our people are signing their death warrant, and you helped them do it!

BOUDINOT
Listen to me, please—!

DROWNING BEAR
Go down there and stop them!

BOUDINOT
Listen to me—!

SCHERMERHORN
Now wait—we're all speaking in the heat of anger, saying things we don't mean. We must all be Christians.

THOMAS
Shut up, you long-legged windbag! You're not talking to a bunch of poor farmers now! Just wait'll Andy Jackson hears about this!
SCHERMERHORN
(*Loftily.*)
I didn't mean to offend anybody. No hard feelings.
(*Turning to go, followed by Reed and Boudinot.*)
May the Lord bless you!
THOMAS
(*Calling after him.*)
May the Lord bless you too, you swindler!
(*The lights go down, and the music rises in a mood of restless intensity.*)

SCENE 8

NARRATOR
Washington in 1836—the forces of American destiny were confused. There was one big political party, with Andrew Jackson in power. That same year Henry Clay and Daniel Webster organized a Whig party to fight Jackson, who had now been President for seven years. And, there was talk of states' rights, of the slave question, of the industrial North squeezing the agricultural South. The very air was charged with a strange, grim kind of unrest. No one had time to think much about the Indian question. The Cherokee country seemed far off. And anyway, didn't the land belong to the white giants?
(*The lights come up on the small stage at audience right, showing the interior of a conference room in the White House— a table down center, a window, a door on the left. At the table sits Lewis Cass. Back of him is Sam Houston. At left is Daniel Webster, and at the right are Junaluska and John Ross. Houston is pacing up and down.*)

HOUSTON

Mr. Cass, we're wastin' time. When's Andy Jackson comin'?

CASS

The President said he would stop by at two o'clock, as a courtesy to Senator Webster.

WEBSTER

Courtesy to *me*?

CASS

After all, this matter is closed.

HOUSTON

Closed? You're crazy!

CASS

Congress authorized us to draw up a treaty and move the Cherokee to the West. The Indians signed the treaty, and that's that.

HOUSTON

Sure!—a bunch of ignorant dummies were tricked into signing it! This whole thing is a scheme to get those frontier people to vote for the Democrat party!

CASS

(*Coolly.*)

That's what the Whigs say, Mr. Houston, but there's nothing political about it. It's been under study for years. There's no other solution to the problem.

HOUSTON

What problem? The Cherokee ain't botherin' nobody! They got their own constitution—they got their own written language that Sequoyah figgered out for 'em—they got their own newspaper, their own churches and schools—they work their farms and live in peace! What's the problem?

JUNALUSKA

Wait—the President will listen. He will listen to Junaluska.

CASS

Here he comes now.

(Cass rises as the door at left opens and Jackson enters.)

JACKSON

What's goin' on in here? I heard you shoutin' clear down the hall! Howdy, Sam, how's Texas?

HOUSTON

Howdy, Mr. President.

JACKSON

(Glancing at Webster then turning away.)

Cass, I see you got Senator Webster all riled up again.

(Webster turns away in exasperation as Jackson crosses toward the others.)

Howdy, Ross.

(Shaking hands.)

Well, well—Junaluska! After twenty years! I haven't seen you since Horseshoe Bend.

(Junaluska shakes hands and nods gravely.)

WEBSTER

Mr. President, this treaty—

JACKSON

(Sitting down.)

What about the treaty?

HOUSTON

It was put through by a gang of crooks! Those people didn't know what they were signing! Not one Cherokee in fifty attended that meeting!

WEBSTER

It appears, Mr. President, that the Cherokee are being cheated out of their land.

JACKSON

(A little irritated.)

Mr. Cass here is Secretary of War. The report I got from the War Department said the Cherokee voted to sell their land.

WEBSTER

Mr. President, even the Secretary of War wrote that he

would not sanction the methods used by this—this Schermerhorn!

CASS

(*With a start.*)
How did you know that?

WEBSTER

Never mind that now. Mr. President, I have a letter—
(*Drawing it out and unfolding it.*)
I would like to read you a part of it. It was written by a certain Major Davis, of the U. S. Army, to the Secretary of War.

CASS

(*Indignant.*)
Mr. President, I protest! I don't know how the Senator manages to get into the secret files of the War Department —

JACKSON

Let him read it.

WEBSTER

(*Reading.*)
"I now warn you and the President that if this paper of Schermerhorn's called a treaty is sent to the Senate and ratified, you will bring trouble upon the government and eventually destroy the Cherokee nation. The Cherokee are a peaceable, harmless people, but you may drive them to desperation, and this treaty cannot be carried into effect except by the strong arm of force."

(*Earnestly.*)
Do you realize what this means?

JACKSON

(*Stubbornly.*)
The Indians signed a treaty to move out!

ROSS

Excuse me, Mr. President—a little handful of troublemakers signed that paper without knowing what it was and without asking the General Council. Does the United

Above, Drowning Bear (Lawrence Peerce) denounces Boudinot as a traitor. *Below*, Andrew Jackson (Artus Moser) refuses to help the Cherokee.

Above, Wilani (Eileen Smith) tells Mrs. Perkins (Irene Bewley) of Nundayeli's marriage. *Below*, Ann Worcester (Anne Martin) shows Nundayeli (Ethelyn Saloli) the wedding dress.

Above, The square dance before the wedding of Suyeta and Nundayeli. *Below*, Will Thomas (Robert Tedder) plays a prank on Tsali (John Shearin).

Above, Will Thomas reads the army order for the removal of the Cherokee. *Below*, The Lieutenant (Donald Treat) hands payment to one of the villagers.

States government actually recognize deals of this kind? Why, the whole thing was carefully planned to defraud us! Hundreds of lawsuits are already being filed!

JACKSON

(*Puzzled.*)
What kind of lawsuits?

ROSS

White men say the land is now government property. They file claims on it, then charge us rent on our own homes! If we can't pay, they sue us in court.

JACKSON

Well, they can't collect it.

ROSS

Sir, the word of an Indian is no good in court unless it is sworn to by at least two white men! Our people are being robbed!

CASS

Oh, well, you always find a few crooks trying to swindle people out of their money. That happens everywhere, not just with Indians. Now up in Michigan a few years back—

JUNALUSKA

Mr. President, my people are not safe in their homes! The very lowest classes of white men break in and beat our people with hickories, cowhides, and clubs!

JACKSON

(*Impatiently.*)
Well, we got laws, ain't we? Why don't you call in a constable?

JUNALUSKA

Mr. President, the magistrates and constables are the worst of all! They stand and look on while our women are raped and beaten, stripped bare and flogged without mercy, like animals!

(*With deep feeling.*)
Mr. President, send troops to protect us! We shall be broken unless something is done!

CASS
I find this rather hard to believe!

JACKSON
Well, dang it, it's a matter for the state militia.
(*Speaking sardonically to Webster.*)
Ain't that what Senator Calhoun would say?

WEBSTER
(*Grimly.*)
The state militia happens to be involved also! John Ross was arrested at his home in Tennessee by Georgia Guards —taken to jail across the line in Georgia! Surely you read the newspaper stories by John Howard Payne!

JACKSON
(*Turning away with a frown of annoyance.*)
Well—it's outa my hands!
(*Junaluska starts toward him, then stops and breathes deeply.*)

HOUSTON
Outa your hands?

JACKSON
That's what I said!

HOUSTON
(*Hotly.*)
This ain't like you! I've seen you play politics before—even played politics with you—but not this way!

JACKSON
Who's playin' politics? What do you expect me to do?—bring 'em here and put 'em in the White House?

ROSS
Mr. President, before this treaty is sent to Congress, why don't you visit the Cherokee country and see if we're telling the truth?

JACKSON
Do you think I've got time to go traipsin' off down there? I been dealin' with Indians all my life. The investigation's

been made already, by all of us, for the last two hundred years! Nobody can tell them anything about Indians!

WEBSTER

This is contrary to every principle of American democracy! I'll fight it as long as I have a breath in my body!

JACKSON

(*Rising angrily.*)

Now you listen to me, all of you! The people of this country elected me president so I'd look after their interests, and not throw away the taxpayers' money on a lot of scrubby mountain land! Mr. Webster and his Whigs in the Senate can preach all day about justice, and humanity, and civil rights—but the Cherokee have been offered a fair price—they voted to sell—and that's that!

(*In a rage.*)

Is there anything else?

JUNALUSKA

(*Grimly.*)

One thing more, Mr. President.

JACKSON

Well?

JUNALUSKA

The Cherokee would like to become citizens of the United States.

(*Jackson stares at him, grunts in amazement, turns toward the door, then stops and looks at Junaluska.*)

JACKSON

Far as I'm concerned, the Cherokee are movin' to Oklahoma!

(*He goes out and slams the door. The others stand in awed silence for a moment. Junaluska clenches his fists.*)

JUNALUSKA

(*Bitterly.*)

If Junaluska had known this was going to happen, he

would never have saved Jackson's life that day at Horseshoe Bend!

(The lights go down; the music rises in a sombre mood.)

SCENE 9

Narrator

Junaluska and John Ross stayed in Washington and went on fighting for the Cherokee. A year went by—then two —and Junaluska had gone back and forth to Washington several times. The Cherokee newspaper—*The Phoenix*—said the treaty might never get through Congress, because all over the East white citizens were rising up in protest.

(The lights come up on the center stage, showing a village. There is a house up right, and a church up left from which comes the sound of a choir singing "Amazing Grace." Down center sits Wilani, sewing on a pink dress.)

It was now 1838. Again Junaluska had gone to Washington, because now it seemed that the battle was won. In the meantime, here in the valleys of the Great Smokies, spring came in all its ancient glory, and life flowed on as usual.

(As Wilani turns partly toward the right to hold up the dress and examine it, Tsali comes in from the left, stops and looks at her, then tiptoes quickly across and behind her. He has a wheatstraw in his hand, and he leans forward and tickles the back of her neck with the straw. She brushes it away and goes on working. Tsali smiles and tickles her again, and again she brushes it away. The third time she turns and sees him; they both laugh, then he hurries to her and kneels on one knee beside her to look at the dress. She puts her arm around his neck, just as Mrs. Perkins comes out of the house up right.)

MRS. PERKINS

Lord help us, Wilani, I ain't been so excited since my own weddin' thirty years ago! Just think—Nundayeli all grown up and gettin' married! Church weddin', too! She'll be the prettiest bride in this whole country!

TSALI

No—not like Wilani.
    (*Wilani smiles as he takes her hand.*)

MRS. PERKINS

Well, anyway, you ought to be proud to have such a beautiful daughter.

WILANI

Tsali is proud. You remember that day he came back from Horseshoe Bend? He wanted many sons. Now he has sons, but he is more proud of Nundayeli than any of them!

MRS. PERKINS

Well, why not? What good is a bunch of old awkward boys?

WILANI

    (*Examining the dress.*)
Do you think this neck is too low?

MRS. PERKINS

Well—I don't know—looks all right to me—
    (*Tsali takes hold of the dress to examine it, then draws back as Wilani slaps his hand smartly.*)
—we can try it and see.
    (*Calling toward the house.*)
Nundayeli? Come try on the dress!
    (*Again Tsali tries to touch the dress and Wilani holds it away from him.*)
Keep your big hands offa that dress, Tsali. Do you want to ruin it?

NUNDAYELI

    (*Coming out of the house, a fresh, beautiful Indian girl.*)

My hair won't do right! I've brushed it a dozen times. How does it look?

Mrs. Perkins

Oh, it looks fine. And here's the dress!

(*Nundayeli stops and gazes in awe as Wilani holds up the dress. She smiles, takes it gently, rubs it a moment then presses it against her cheek. Ann Worcester, a pretty young white woman, comes out of the church and crosses the stage.*)

Ann

Well, how does it look? Can you make it fit?

Nundayeli

Oh, Ann!

Mrs. Perkins

It's the prettiest dress I ever saw!

Ann

Well, it's been made over at least a dozen times.

Nundayeli

I never saw anything so soft and shiny! It's so pretty I want to cry!

Mrs. Perkins

Cryin's bad luck! If any cryin's gonna be done, I'll do it.

Wilani

Wilani would like to cry—because she is so happy.

(*Again she looks at Tsali, and he takes her hand with a smile.*)

Ann

(*Laughing.*)

No one's going to cry! This is supposed to be a happy day! And besides, every bride who wears this dress lives a long, happy life. Just look at my great-grandmother—she lived to be eighty-six, and had eleven children. Just think—on her wedding day a present came from Queen Anne! That was in 1712, over a hundred years ago!

Nundayeli

Were you named after Queen Anne?

ANN

Yes—and so was my mother, and my grandmother. On the day Queen Anne sent that wedding gift, my great-grandmother made a vow that all her descendants would be named Anne.

MRS. PERKINS

All of 'em?

ANN

(*Laughing.*)
Well—only the girls! Anyway, the dress brings good luck, and I'm glad you can wear it, Nundayeli.

WILANI

For ten years you make us very happy, Ann Worcester. But your ancestors in England were great people, and now you live with the poor Cherokee far away in the mountains. Why?

ANN

I go with my husband.

WILANI

Sam Worcester had a fine church in Massachusetts. Why did he come here?

ANN

(*Simply.*)
Because he is a Christian.

WILANI

(*Nodding with a smile.*)
Yes—and now Tsali is a Christian, and Wilani, and Drowning Bear—all of us. The old ceremonies are gone forever—now we are like everyone else—it is good! Our children will be married in a Christian church!

MRS. PERKINS

(*Glancing toward the left.*)
Not if we don't get that dress on Nundayeli! People are comin' already. Look, they're gonna have a square dance!

ANN

Hurry, Nundayeli! I'll bring the dress!

(The four women hurry into the house up right, and Tsali backs upstage out of the way, smiling and waving to the crowd. The dancers, both white and Indians, rush in from the left, laughing and joking. The music starts up in a typical square dance tune, as the leader hastily gets the circle organized with "Choose your partners," "Make a circle," etc. As the dance begins in color and gayety, other villagers saunter onto the scene—Will Thomas, Drowning Bear, Sam Worcester, Tsali's sons, and others watching the dance and clapping their hands in time with the music. As the dance comes to a climax, Thomas, at a nod from Worcester, stops the dance.)

THOMAS

All right, everybody! Time for the wedding! Time for the wedding! Are you ready, Sam Worcester?

WORCESTER

(Smiling.)

My wife has made over her dress for Nundayeli, and the groom here is wearing my other suit. I guess we'll have to marry 'em so we can get our clothes back!

(He indicates Suyeta, who is wedged into a tight black suit. The people laugh and applaud.)

THOMAS

All right—the first thing will be a speech from that great orator, the father of the bridegroom—Chief Drowning Bear!

DROWNING BEAR

(Stepping out proudly.)

Drowning Bear is not very good at making speeches, but since you asked me to say a few words—

THOMAS

(Interrupting.)

Thank you, Drowning Bear! Fine speech!

(The people laugh and applaud. Drowning Bear steps back with a shrug and a laugh.)

And now a few remarks from the father of the bride—Tsali!

TSALI

(*Proudly.*)
We want everybody to have a good time, and we also want—

THOMAS

Fine speech, Tsali! Thank you!

(*As the people laugh and applaud, the door of the house up right opens, and Nundayeli appears, dressed in the wedding gown, along with Wilani, Mrs. Perkins, and Ann Worcester. They come slowly toward the center as the people step back with murmurs of admiration and excitement.*)

THOMAS

Well! Is the bride ready?

(*As Nundayeli nods, Drowning Bear suddenly steps out and points off left.*)

DROWNING BEAR

Wait—who's this?

(*From the left enters Major Davis, in army uniform. He stops and surveys the scene.*)

DAVIS

I'm Major Davis, U. S. Army. I'm looking for the chief.

DROWNING BEAR

(*Hurrying forward with outstretched hand.*)
Welcome to our village! My name is Drowning Bear! This is my son, Suyeta, and this is my adopted son, Will Thomas.

DAVIS

(*Trying to interrupt.*)
Yes—I see—

DROWNING BEAR

This is Tsali, and that is his wife, Wilani. And this is their daughter, Nundayeli! Why, you're just in time for the

wedding! And this is our missionary, Sam Worcester—and this is his wife, Ann—Mrs. Ann Worcester—and—
> (*He stops in astonishment as Junaluska appears from the right.*)

And this is Junaluska!—the father of our people.
> (*Hurrying across to him.*)

He's just come from Washington! He talked to the President! Now he will tell us the good news!
> (*Junaluska gazes sadly at him and turns away.*)

Davis
> (*Crossing to him, cap in hand.*)

Wait—I've got to talk to you.

Drowning Bear
Junaluska!—what is it?

Davis
I've got three troops of cavalry in this section—one up the road a piece, one over at Stekoah, and one at Cheowa.
> (*A murmur of dread runs through the crowd.*)

Drowning Bear
Cavalry? Little Will, what does he mean?
> (*Davis takes from his cap a folded paper and hands it to Drowning Bear. The other takes it, unfolds it quickly, reads, then suddenly stiffens in grim anger and crumples the paper.*)

No! No!

Thomas
What is it?
> (*He grabs the paper, uncrumples it, then reads aloud.*)

"New Echota, Georgia, May Tenth, 1838, Headquarters Brigadier General Winfield Scott, U. S. Army, to Major James Davis, U. S. Army. You will proceed at once with three troops of cavalry to the Cherokee country in western North Carolina in the vicinity of the Tennessee and Georgia borders. There you will gather the members of the Cherokee nation and transfer them to the Indian territory west of the Mississippi, in the vicinity of Sallisaw, Oklahoma Territory."

(*The people murmur in awe, then listen tensely.*)
"You will collect all men, women, and children into one central location, then move them to Chattanooga to await further orders. You will have the North Carolina portion of the Cherokee nation in Chattanooga not later than June Tenth, 1838."

(*The people become more excited, some of them hurrying to and fro.*)
Why, that's only two weeks!

(*Davis stands in silence as the crowd becomes angry.*)

MRS. PERKINS

That ain't right! The Cherokee are friends of ours! It ain't right!

WHITE MAN

No!

(*Others shout "No!"*)

WORCESTER

You can't take their homes and drive them away like this!

ANOTHER MAN

Who do you think you are?

MRS. PERKINS

Why don't you take us, too?

(*The people are shouting in protest as Davis turns, a little embarrassed, and hurries out at left. The lights go down, leaving a glow on the faces of the people as they gaze after the army officer. The organ rises in a strong chord and moves quickly to a heavy, tragic climax, as the lights go down.*)

Act Two

SCENE 1

(For a brief interlude the organ and choir join in a noble, majestic strain of music, expressing at the same time a sense of tragedy and impending doom, the struggle of humanity trapped by inexorable fate.)

NARRATOR

Out of the great womb of destiny, into the doorway of the world, come the souls of men, created equal in the sight of God. When their day is done, they return still equal, into the bosom of the Eternal. Somewhere between, on the plains of human life, caught in the monstrous mistakes that men devise to plague each other, it is the fate of some people to undergo pain and death, and to be twisted on the rack of greed and hatred.

The Cherokee were beginning to realize that at last their time had come. A dark frenzy tore into the minds of the people. Like summer lightning the news shot through the mountains, down the green valleys. The Cherokee had been left alone for so long now that they had almost forgotten the fateful treaty which a handful of their brothers had foolishly accepted in the name of the Cherokee nation. The Indians had so many friends among the white people that this terrible thing did not seem possible. But it was true. And now it was upon them.

(The music ceases and the lights come up on the center stage, where people are moving to and fro in a restless kind of confusion. A column of people approaches from the right. The leaders are being stopped at a table down right, where a lieutenant is counting out money and checking names on a list. Across center to the left are two constables, who are serving warrants and taking back most of the money. The people pass slowly off at left, dejected, while all

along the stage they are comforted and consoled by Will Thomas, Drowning Bear, and Sam Worcester. Soldiers are posted along the way to keep the column moving.)

LIEUTENANT

(Counting out money to an Indian.)

Twenty, forty, fifty, fifty-five, fifty-six—fifty-six dollars and thirty-eight cents.

(Handing it to the man.)

There you are.

(The man shakes his head, while his wife tugs at him in warning.)

Here, take it!

(The man still refuses.)

What's the matter now? You expecting something for your house and barn, all of them cattle?

(The man nods.)

Well, you won't get any more. Each person gets fifty-six dollars and thirty-eight cents. Your wife's got hers; now take yours and move along!

(The man stands stubbornly. The Lieutenant slams the money down on the table.)

Take it and stop wasting time!

(Will Thomas hurries across, picks up the money, and gives it to the man, pats him on the shoulder, then leads him across toward the left. The constables meet him and the woman, produce their papers, then take most of the money. Meanwhile another man is at the table down right.)

I can't find your name here. You must not own any land.

(The man nods vigorously.)

Well, your name's not here! This is the list of all the members of the Cherokee nation. If your name's not here, I can't pay you. Move on!

(The man turns away dejectedly. Thomas rushes to the table.)

THOMAS

That man was not paid! What's wrong?

LIEUTENANT

Stand aside!

THOMAS

I demand to see that list! Why are you holding back some of the money?

LIEUTENANT

Get away, or I'll have you arrested!

(*In the meantime Major Davis has hurried in from the right. Thomas calls to him, but Davis waves him aside and goes to the constables at left.*)

DAVIS

What are you men doing here?

CONSTABLE

Collectin' debts from these here Indians. We got warrants on 'em from every magistrate in this end o' the state, I reckon. Hafta get the money while they got it!

DAVIS

What are the warrants for?

CONSTABLE

(*With a shrug.*)

Rent, mostly.

DAVIS

(*Frowning.*)

Rent?

CONSTABLE

They owe nearly three years rent!

DAVIS

Rent on their own homes? What are you talking about?

CONSTABLE

Aw, this ain't their land, Major! It belongs to the government.

DAVIS

(*Indignantly.*)

We're buying it from them, aren't we?

CONSTABLE
Well, I reckon that's just a formality to keep 'em quiet. Claims on these lands was filed more'n three years ago. These people should've moved off then, when we first told 'em.

DAVIS
(*Growing angry.*)
Who claims the land?

CONSTABLE
White people.

DAVIS
By what right?

CONSTABLE
(*Irritated.*)
Squatters' rights! The government's declared 'em public lands!

DAVIS
(*Whirling angrily to the lieutenant.*)
Who let these vultures in here?

LIEUTENANT
Why—I did, sir. I thought—

DAVIS
(*Turning again to the constables.*)
Get outa here, you damn buzzards! Get out!

CONSTABLE
Now wait a minute! We got warrants to serve!

DAVIS
Get out!

CONSTABLE
We ain't doin' nothin' wrong! We got the law on our side!
(*The second constable tries to pull him away.*)

DAVIS
Get away, and stay away!

(*He grabs the money box from the man's hands with a rough jerk.*)

Give me that money box. Now take your crooked warrants and get away from here!

(*He turns to the Lieutenant and hands him the box.*)

CONSTABLE

Give me that money!

DAVIS

Lieutenant, if these tramps show up here again, I want 'em arrested!

LIEUTENANT

Yes, sir!

DAVIS

Now get out!

(*A soldier moves closer to the constables and levels his rifle.*)

CONSTABLE

We'll just see about this, mister! You're robbin' an officer of the law and obstructin' justice! This is a free country! You can't take the law in your own hands!

(*The second man keeps pointing to the rifles and urging the first constable to keep quiet.*)

DAVIS

This section is under martial law. If you're not out of this village in three minutes, I'll have you both thrown in that stockade! Now get out and stay out!

(*The two men back out at left, glowering and muttering. Davis takes the box from the Lieutenant and motions to Drowning Bear.*)

Chief, take this down to the stockade and give it back to the people. They don't have to give one cent to those buzzards!

DROWNING BEAR

(*Gratefully.*)

Thank you, Major!

(*He and Thomas go out quickly at left. The stage is now clear, except for the soldiers, Major Davis, and*

Above, Wilani (Eileen Smith) falls and is goaded by a drunken soldier (Gordon Peters). *Below,* The body of Wilani is carried away after she is brutally killed.

Above, Tsali (John Shearin) jeers at the trickery of the white man. *Below,* Tsali tells Major Davis (Bernard Barrow) that he has come to give his life for his people.

Above, Tsali and his two sons are lead away by the firing squad. *Below,* Boudinot (Arsene Thompson) prays after the martyr, Tsali, is led to his execution.

Above, William Henry Harrison (W. P. Covington, III) promises Drowning Bear (Lawrence Peerce) protection for the Cherokee. *Below,* The dying Junaluska (Ross Durfee) returns.

the missionary, Sam Worcester, who walks about anxiously in the background. Davis turns back toward the table down right, takes off his cap wearily.)

DAVIS

I saw General Scott this morning, and he's pretty mad. Is everything all right here?

LIEUTENANT

Yes, sir—except that white fellow, Thomas, keeps harping about some of the names not being on the list.

DAVIS

Well, why aren't they on the list?

LIEUTENANT

I don't know, sir. It's the list we got from Washington.

DAVIS

Well—you pay 'em anyway.

LIEUTENANT

But, sir, we'll run out of money!

DAVIS

(Impatiently.)
Then we'll have to get more! You pay every one of them!
(Reflecting.)
They're not getting anything now for their houses and barns—

LIEUTENANT

Well, they're just log cabins, most of them.

DAVIS

(Sharply.)
What difference does that make?
(Coming to the table.)
How many have you paid so far?

LIEUTENANT

About twenty-five in this section, sir. We're almost finished.

DAVIS

Twenty-five? This valley has at least fifty people! Where are all the rest?

LIEUTENANT

Hiding in the mountains, sir.

DAVIS

Confound it, I told you to get all of them!

LIEUTENANT

Sir, how do you expect anybody to find an Indian hiding in these mountains?

DAVIS

Now you listen to me! I have strict orders from General Winfield Scott—

(*Junaluska enters hurriedly from the left.*)

JUNALUSKA

Major Davis!

DAVIS

Well?

JUNALUSKA

Please do something!—our people are jammed in that stockade like cattle!

DAVIS

They may have to live in stockades for weeks. I can't build a house for each one!

JUNALUSKA

Well, that's no reason for whipping them!

DAVIS

(*Whirling on the Lieutenant.*)

Whipping?

LIEUTENANT

(*Defensively.*)

Nobody's been whipped unless they started trouble!

JUNALUSKA

Why can't you treat them like human beings?

Davis

You tell them to behave like human beings!—dozens of them hiding out in the mountains!—from this one valley alone!

Junaluska

How can you expect them to do anything else?

Davis

All right! Every man who hides out will be shot on sight! They're all outlaws!

Junaluska

Outlaws? Because they do not want to give up their homes?

Davis

That's what I said!

> (*Irritated, he hurries out at left, followed by Junaluska. At far right another group of refugees enters, led by a drunken soldier who is shoving and mistreating an old woman, muttering for her to move faster. She drops her pack and the soldier growls at her to pick it up.*)

Worcester

> (*Hurrying across toward the right.*)

Wilani!

> (*Junaluska enters from the left, then runs across. Worcester stops him and holds him back.*)

Junaluska

Stop it! Stop it!

Drunken Soldier

Go on—pick it up!

> (*Wilani gets the pack up once more, staggers forward, then falls again as the soldier gives her a shove.*)

Junaluska

She can't carry it! She needs help!

Lieutenant

You keep your nose out of this!

Junaluska
Do something! That soldier's drunk!

Drunken Soldier
I told you to pick it up!

(He staggers a moment.)

All right—I been tellin' you—now I'll show you!

(He raises his rifle and brings the butt down heavily at Wilani's head. There is a cry, then she is still. Tsali, meanwhile, has been struggling to get loose from two soldiers behind. He tears himself free with a jerk, rushes to Wilani, and drops to his knees beside her. He examines her nervously for a moment, then he looks around, finds a rock, and suddenly leaps to his feet and beats the drunken soldier over the head. The soldier collapses, and Tsali, with a cry, turns and runs out of sight up the valley at right, followed by three others. The soldiers run to the right.)

Lieutenant
Stop those men! Stop them!

(Several shots are fired. Immediately a crowd of the villagers rushes in from the left, then Major Davis follows them in.)

Worcester
(Examining the two figures.)
They're both dead!

Junaluska
(In horror.)
Dead!

Davis
(Rushing across to the right.)
What's going on? What was that firing?

Lieutenant
Some of the Indians escaped.

Davis
Escaped? How?

WORCESTER

(*Sternly.*)
One of your men was drunk!

DAVIS

(*Suddenly enraged.*)
Drunk?

LIEUTENANT

(*Angry and embarrassed.*)
He was trying to make an old woman move along. She fell, and I guess she died of exhaustion. One of the Indians hit our man and killed him. Four Indians got away.

DAVIS

(*Controlling his rage.*)
Was that man drunk?

LIEUTENANT

I guess so.

DAVIS

You ignorant fool! Get out of here! Go down there and guard that stockade! Sergeant, take over here!
(*To the Lieutenant, who is hesitating.*)
Get out! Get out!
(*The Lieutenant crosses angrily and goes out at left. Davis comes to the center and glares at the people.*)
I ought to tie every blasted one of you to a tree! That's four more outlaws—and they killed an American soldier! Someone will have to pay for this!

THOMAS

(*Hotly.*)
Are you crazy? That man got what he deserved!

DAVIS

I'll lock every blamed one of them in that stockade 'til hell freezes over! I let them out for a little while, and they come running up here like a bunch of wild horses. I'm getting sick and tired of this!
(*He turns to Junaluska, who stands at right in silence.*)

You're supposed to be the great leader, the big patriarch —well, why don't you make them act right?

 (*Junaluska stands in silence.*)

Standing there like a stump—why don't you do something?

 (*Exasperated, Davis hurries past him to the scene at right.*)

Sergeant, take that body back to headquarters. Tell them I said send a wagon to New Echota.

 (*The soldiers carry off the body of the other at far right. Junaluska follows Davis back to the center.*)

JUNALUSKA

 (*With great feeling.*)

Major Davis! My people will do whatever they are told to do—but they are human beings, not animals! When they suffer, they fight back! They are not cowards! If you treat them right, there will be no trouble, I promise you! But if you must kill, then take Junaluska and kill him—but do not hurt my people!

DAVIS

Now you listen to me! I didn't choose to do this! The President of the United States has ordered us to move the Cherokee to the West. There are more than fifteen thousand in this country, and every time one man escapes, it makes the whole thing harder—do you understand?

JUNALUSKA

I understand that the Cherokee are kind and gentle! All they want is to live in peace! Their homes are taken away—they are driven a thousand miles into a new country—do you think each one will lay down everything and walk away without feeling hurt and bitter? They are human beings!

 (*Two of the villagers at right are carrying out the body of Wilani.*)

You tie their hands, march them like cattle, throw them in stockades in the hot sun—you beat them, starve them—

 (*Pointing.*)

You even let your drunken soldiers kill them!
(*Almost overcome.*)
Major Davis—Junaluska knows there is nothing the Cherokee can do! There is no hope anywhere! But my people are a great race! They fought and died to help save this nation for you! They have courage and honor—let them keep that honor!

Davis
(*Trying to control his anger.*)
All through this country men are hiding in the mountains—I have orders to stop it!
(*A pause, then firmly.*)
I want those men brought back here!
(*The people murmur excitedly.*)

Junaluska
Tsali and his three sons?

Davis
They killed an American soldier!

Drowning Bear
(*Quivering with rage.*)
The soldier killed Tsali's wife!

Davis
That's not the point! I want those men brought back here as an example to the rest. I've got to stop this running away and hiding.

Thomas
What about the others who ran away before Tsali?
(*Davis takes a deep breath, looks at the others.*)

Davis
All right—I'll make a bargain with you—get those four men back here, and we'll forget about the rest.

Junaluska
Will you give Tsali a fair trial?

Davis
(*Firmly.*)

He'll be put before a firing squad.
>(*Drowning Bear leaps forward as the people murmur in excitement.*)

>>DROWNING BEAR

No! Tsali is innocent!

>>DAVIS

>(*Gazing steadily at Junaluska.*)

Well—what do you say?

>>JUNALUSKA

>(*Bitterly.*)

Tsali's home has been taken, his land, his freedom. His wife has been murdered! Now you ask him to give his own life—and his three sons! Do you enjoy seeing our people die?
>(*Davis seems unable to face Junaluska, and he turns away, apparently confused and embarrassed. Junaluska turns slowly to Drowning Bear.*)

Drowning Bear will go to the mountains—and search out the hiding place of Tsali.

>>DROWNING BEAR

>(*Turning away in anger.*)

Do not ask Drowning Bear to do this! Tsali is my best friend!

>>JUNALUSKA

Will Thomas will go with Drowning Bear. Little Will knows every cave on Clingman's Dome.

>>THOMAS

Do you think Tsali is crazy? He will never come back! Why should he? He'll die in the mountains first! I can't do it, Junaluska!

>>JUNALUSKA

Drowning Bear will go now—and take Will Thomas. He will speak to Tsali, in the name of his people. He will ask Tsali and his sons to come back—and die.
>(*The lights go down slowly and the music begins in a pastoral background.*)

SCENE 2

(The lights come up on the small stage at audience left, showing a cave in the mountains in mid-afternoon. Upstage right sits one of the sons with a rifle across his lap. Up left a small boy sits watching his father. Down center Tsali and the other son are performing a prayer-like ritual, a primitive half-dance and half-ceremony in a series of slow movements, dignified and solemn. Tsali and the son spread a blanket on the ground. Then Tsali stands back of it and raises one arm slowly to the heavens. The son follows his movements at the other side of the blanket. As the Narrator speaks, the ritual is continued, with Tsali finally watching as the son performs alone.)

NARRATOR

From the base of the east,
From the doorway of the rainbow,
At the fore part of my house within the dawn,
The sun god sits with me.
Beautifully my fire to me is restored.
In beauty may I walk,
I and my sons all day through the returning glory.
On the trail marked with pollen may we walk,
In old age wandering on a trail of beauty—
Living again may we walk.
It is finished in beauty.

(The music stops. Suddenly Tsali shakes his head angrily, seizes the blanket and flings it defiantly on the ground, then turns slowly upstage and sits on one of the boulders at the mouth of the cave. The small lad comes near and sits by him, and Tsali puts his arm around him. The son downstage gathers the blanket and brings it to Tsali, who takes it reverently and holds it in his lap. The son at right hears a noise in the woods and starts up, leveling his rifle off right. Tsali leaps to his feet, hurries to him, and

peers down the mountainside. He lifts the barrel of the rifle and turns slowly back to the center. Drowning Bear and Will Thomas hurry in from the right and stop to survey the scene. Thomas crosses to the right as Drowning Bear comes near Tsali down center.)

Tsali

(Without turning.)
Where is Wilani?

Drowning Bear

At my house. The people brought flowers and pine branches. They placed her so the evening sun would fall across her face. Will Thomas brought a red and yellow dress from his store—

Tsali

Wilani always wanted a red and yellow dress, but Tsali was always too poor. Wilani said nothing, but all these years Tsali knew—and Will Thomas knew. Wilani worked hard all her life. Now she can rest. She knows Tsali is not a murderer.

(As if to himself.)
When the soldiers came, Wilani did not cry. She waked the boys, cooked breakfast for the soldiers and then for us. She wanted to milk the cows, but the soldiers said to hurry. As we went down the path, the cows bawled. Wilani looked back and cried because there was no one to milk the cows.

(Drowning Bear comes to Tsali and takes the blanket from him, tosses it into the bushes. Tsali watches him, then bows his head.)

Drowning Bear

Reverend Sam Worcester will have a service at Drowning Bear's house tomorrow at sundown. She will have a *Christian* burial.

Tsali

Tsali will be there.
(Drowning Bear glances at Thomas. Tsali senses something is wrong.)

Drowning Bear wears a strange face! What is it?
####### THOMAS
You can't come to the funeral.
####### TSALI
Why not?
####### THOMAS
Any man hiding in the mountains is an outlaw. You'd be shot on sight.
####### TSALI
(*With sudden anger.*)
Tsali will be there! After that no man will ever see us again! We will go to the west fork of Deep Creek! Soldiers will never come there!
(*There is a strained silence as the others turn away.*)
You still have strange faces! You think Tsali is a murderer?
####### THOMAS
No!
####### TSALI
Why did you come? Did the white man send you?
(*Drowning Bear turns away quickly.*)
It's true! They sent you!
(*Rushing to Thomas, seizing him and rubbing his cheek roughly.*)
White! White! Always white men bring death to the Cherokee! They killed Tsali's father, and his two brothers—they killed Wilani! Now they want to kill Tsali and his three sons! They are like mad dogs! Tsali hates white men!
(*He spits angrily and leaps upstage.*)
Let them come and get us!
(*Beating his chest.*)
Tell them where we are, Will Thomas! Tell them to come!
####### DROWNING BEAR
Drowning Bear has a message.
####### TSALI
Give the message—then go!

Drowning Bear
The white general says all those in the mountains can go free—if Tsali and his three sons will come back.
> (*Tsali is startled.*)

The white general says he cannot find all those in the mountains. He must make an example to the people. If Tsali will give up and be—punished—the rest of our people can stay in the mountains.

Tsali
The white general is very proud!
> (*A sudden thought comes to him.*)

It's a trick! Yes, it's a trick!
> (*To the son with the rifle.*)

You hear, Kanega! It's a trick to make us come back! They never keep their word! They will kill us like rabbits, and the others too! That's it! No—we will not go! Tell the white general we will not come back!

Drowning Bear
> (*Embarrassed and bitter.*)

Drowning Bear has another message.
> (*Tsali turns away.*)

Many years ago, before the great Sequoyah went away, the Cherokee promised to live in peace.

Tsali
Tsali made no promise! He was not there! Sequoyah is gone—let the west wind scatter the dust of his bones! Go—Tsali has no more words!

Drowning Bear
> (*Torn between friendship and duty.*)

The great Junaluska gave his word to Sequoyah!
> (*Tsali is visibly moved, but he stands stubbornly looking away. Drowning Bear speaks almost wildly.*)

Junaluska has spoken to the white general. The white general says he will be kind to the Cherokee if Tsali will do as he says. Junaluska said—in the name of Sequoyah, in the name of our people—tell Tsali to come back.

Tsali
(*Overcome with anger and bitterness.*)
It is wrong! Tsali and his people have been ground to pieces by the white man! Now Junaluska says come back! It is wrong! Tsali loves his sons!
> (*He sinks down on the boulder upstage and buries his face in his hands. Drowning Bear watches him for a moment in grief and despair, then motioning to Thomas he hurries out at right, followed quickly by Thomas. The three sons come to Tsali and stand close to him as the lights go down.*)

SCENE 3

> (*Before the lights come up the choir can be heard singing "Amazing Grace." The dull glow of early morning is mingled on the stage with the red of two campfires one down left and one upstage near the church. Down left several soldiers are sprawled on the ground. Upstage are Drowning Bear, Junaluska, and Will Thomas sitting in silence around the fire. As the scene progresses, the rising lights indicate that daylight had come. Major Davis enters from the left and stops before the first campfire.*)

Davis
(*To the soldiers.*)
Good morning men. We'll start moving as soon as it's daylight. You'd better get down to the stockade and help.

First Soldier
(*As the men get to their feet quickly.*)
Looks like the Major ain't had much sleep.

Davis
What about it?

Second Soldier
Maybe the Major's takin' it too hard. After all, they're just a bunch o' Indians!

DAVIS

(*Sharply.*)

Shut up and do as you're told!

SOLDIERS

Yes, sir!

(*They go out at left. Davis saunters upstage to the other campfire, apparently ill at ease.*)

DAVIS

Any word from Tsali?

(*Drowning Bear looks up, then slowly shakes his head. Davis glances at Thomas, then paces slowly with his hands behind his back.*)

Thomas, I understand you've been going to Raleigh for the past few years and buying up this land around here. You've got Drowning Bear living on it, also his son, Suyeta. You leased some land over near Birdtown in their names. How many more?

(*Thomas flings down his knife, with which he has been whittling, and glares defiantly at Davis. Davis seems strangely pleased.*)

Well, anyway, I can't touch them. There's some legal question involved, and now it's up to the State of North Carolina. I guess they'll stay here.

(*He turns and starts out at left, stops, and glances at the three men once more, as if relenting his kindness.*)

The ones in the mountains are still outlaws!

(*He goes out hurriedly at left, as Worcester comes out of the church, rubs his forehead, and saunters totoward the fireplace. He seems to be forcing his good humor.*)

WORCESTER

(*Rubbing his hands.*)

Well, we're just about ready! Ann is packing the things into the wagon out back.

JUNALUSKA

(*Rising.*)

Reverend Sam Worcester is going back to Massachusetts?

WORCESTER

Massachusetts? No.
(*Pacing about.*)
I'm leaving the church just as it is, so the next preacher won't have so much work to do. Drowning Bear, I want you to look after the place—patch the roof, keep the weeds out of the cemetery. I guess we'll take most of the hymn books with us. My wife said she could never give up her choir.

JUNALUSKA

(*Warmly.*)
Reverend Sam Worcester is going to the west?

WORCESTER

Yes. I talked to Ann about it, and she didn't even hesitate. She said, "Of course, we're going. Our place is with the Cherokee." So—that's that! I'll take my wagon and two horses—
(*Smiling and rubbing his hands.*)
—we'll tie a cow to the back of the wagon. We'll use that wagon for a dairy, a church, and a hospital—Will Thomas gave me a load of medicine and liniment.

JUNALUSKA

(*Deeply moved.*)
That is good! You will take the Christian God along with the Cherokee. The heart of Junaluska is glad! Reverend Sam Worcester is our friend, just as Elias Boudinot —is our enemy!

WORCESTER

Just because he has a different point of view? Elias Boudinot is a Cherokee, and he loves his people. Perhaps he is right—perhaps our place is in the West, after all. Anyway—Drowning Bear and Will Thomas will have to find a new preacher.

DROWNING BEAR

Drowning Bear is going to the west himself!

Worcester
No! You've worked hard for many years and saved money to buy your land!

Drowning Bear
A chief's place is with his people.

Junaluska
Some of our people are still here, in the mountains. Your own son, Suyeta, and his wife, Nundayeli—you must stay here and work for them, then some day we can all come back home again. There is no one left but you!

Drowning Bear
They have John Ross—many others. They have Will Thomas.

Junaluska
John Ross and all the other chiefs must go. You are the only one!

Drowning Bear
(*Bitterly.*)
What can one man do? My people are outlaws!

Junaluska
Tsali will come back!

Drowning Bear
No!

Worcester
Did you know, Drowning Bear, that when we started to have the funeral yesterday we found a piece of cloth torn from Wilani's dress?

Drowning Bear
(*Looking up with a start then turning away.*)
That means Tsali will never come back! He will die, like the others, back in the mountains. One by one they will all die!—like the beech trees in the autumn snow—
(*They turn toward the left as someone approaches, then all back away and turn their heads. Worcester crosses toward the house at right as Ann Worcester*

appears in the doorway, then all gaze back toward the left. The crowd of refugees comes in, led by Davis and accompanied by soldiers. Elias Boudinot is at the head of the group. The people fill the left stage, loaded with packs and bundles. Davis holds up his hand and they pause and put down their loads.)

Davis

You people—be ready to leave in ten minutes.
(There is a silence as the group on the stage gazes in sadness at the villagers. Drowning Bear turns away toward the right, then suddenly he gives a start.)

Drowning Bear

Tsali! Tsali!
(He runs toward the right. Tsali and his three sons are approaching the stage. Tsali and Drowning Bear meet for a moment, then Tsali goes on toward Davis as the people murmur in excitement.)

Tsali

(Facing Davis.)
Will the Cherokee in the mountains go free now?

Davis

Yes.

Tsali

Tsali and his sons are ready.
(The people murmur in protest.)

Drowning Bear

No! No! Give Tsali a fair trial! He is innocent! He is innocent!
(Davis hesitates for an instant, then turns to the soldiers down left.)

Davis

Sergeant, you have your orders.
(The soldiers snap to attention, then shoulder their rifles. Ann Worcester steps toward the center from the house up right.)

Ann

Wait!

> (*She comes to the small son of Tsali and pulls him away from the group. Davis is about to protest, then in confusion he turns his back and clenches his fists. Ann and Sam Worcester take the boy across and join the villagers at left. Davis motions to the soldiers, who march briskly across to stage right and stop, facing off right. Davis turns slowly to Tsali.*)

Davis

Do you wish to say anything?

> (*Tsali takes a step forward, then pulls from his belt the strip of torn red and yellow cloth. He gazes down at it for a moment, then turns to the villagers.*)

Tsali

Tsali wants his people to sing!

> (*The people begin rather halfheartedly to sing the old hymn, "Amazing Grace," with Ann Worcester's voice leading them. Tsali and the two sons turn and move inside the two files of soldiers, then the group marches off at right. Davis crosses quickly and stands looking off toward the right while the people move a few steps to the center and peer as they sing. Suddenly the singing breaks off into sobs. Worcester drops to his knees to pray quietly. Junaluska looks at Boudinot, then slowly motions to him. Boudinot kneels and begins to pray in Cherokee. It is the 121st Psalm, which the Narrator, in a low voice in the background, translates to English. Davis again is about to take a step off right. He turns to face Junaluska, lifts his hand a moment as if to speak, then turns toward the house up right, takes off his cap, and leans against the corner of the house. Suddenly there is a volley of shots off right, followed by a deathly stillness. Davis remains motionless with his hand over his eyes. Junaluska steps out, motions to the people. They pick up their*

bundles and start off at the right, led by Junaluska. The music rises in a tragic climax as the lights go down, leaving a glow on the faces of the people. Davis is still leaning against the house with bowed head.)

NARRATOR

West out of the Great Smokies, from village after village, marched seventeen thousand men, women and children, into the setting sun. In the dust of that summer, in the snow and ice of that winter, five thousand people—nearly one-third of the whole Cherokee nation—died and were buried in nameless graves along the Trail of Tears from North Carolina to Oklahoma.

(The lights are out, and the Narrator continues.)

SCENE 4

NARRATOR

The years dragged on. Still faithful to the vision of Sequoyah and Junaluska, the Cherokee back home never gave up the struggle. And there was still one man in Washington who was their friend. In the spring of 1841 Drowning Bear and Will Thomas went to Washington to see that man. He had now been asked to serve as Secretary of State in the cabinet of the new president, William Henry Harrison. Perhaps, they thought, this might be the dawn of a new day. But President Harrison was very ill that morning.

(The lights come up on the small stage at audience right, showing again the interior of the White House conference room. At the table sits Harrison, his shoulders covered with a shawl. At the left are Drowning Bear and Will Thomas. At the right is Daniel Webster.)

WEBSTER

Excuse me for bringing up this matter at this time, Mr. President, but I've got to do it. To me it is one of the

most burning issues we've ever dealt with in this country.
>(*Harrison is watching Drowning Bear, who is shifting uncomfortably from one foot to the other.*)

HARRISON
(*To Drowning Bear.*)
Why, what's the matter?

DROWNING BEAR
(*Sheepishly.*)
New shoes, Mr. President!

HARRISON
Well, take 'em off.

DROWNING BEAR
(*Embarrassed.*)
Not in the house of President Harrison!

HARRISON
Nonsense! We don't stand on ceremony here. Go ahead —take 'em off—here, I'll join you!
>(*He leans down and takes off his shoes, sets them ceremoniously on the table. Drowning Bear then takes off his shoes, murmuring his thanks.*)

There, that's better.
>(*Turning to Webster*).

Now—what were you saying, Daniel?

WEBSTER
Mr. President, the Cherokee were always a nation of mountain farmers. If the government had been wise, these people would still be cultivating those hills and valleys in the Great Smokies. The Removal was a mistake.

HARRISON
Why do you say that, Daniel?

WEBSTER
Mr. President, the ones who stayed behind have become part of the civilization of the whites. They are substantial, inoffensive, law-abiding citizens.

HARRISON

Do you have proof of that?

WEBSTER

I have. There was a certain Major Davis—one of General Winfield Scott's cavalry officers—who took part in the Removal. He later resigned from the army and is now the U. S. District Attorney in Cherokee County, North Carolina. He reports that in the last five years he has prosecuted over five hundred white men in court, and only one Cherokee—and he was led into trouble by a drunken white man!

HARRISON

(*Nodding.*)

Very well, Daniel. What do you want?

WEBSTER

Two things—first, a reservation.

HARRISON

Reservation? Where?

WEBSTER

A section of land in the Great Smokies.

HARRISON

And—the second thing?

WEBSTER

Citizenship.

HARRISON

Citizenship?

(*In awe.*)

That'll be a hard fight, Daniel, especially right now, and you know it! It's unheard of! Why, we're still fighting Indians out west!

WEBSTER

Well, we can start on it. In the meantime, these people want some kind of assurance that they will not be molested.

HARRISON

What do you mean?

THOMAS

The Cherokee are not citizens, Mr. President, therefore they have no right to own property. Actually they have no right even to be there in the Great Smokies, but most of the white people don't seem to mind—they're very friendly. As fast as I get the money, I buy up land and hold it in my name, then lease it to Cherokee families.

HARRISON

Well—what's wrong with that?

THOMAS

There is no legal basis for it, Mr. President. The Cherokee have no protection. They work their farms in peace and never cause any trouble, but there is always some white man who thinks he can take anything in sight as long as it belongs to an Indian.

HARRISON

(*Reflecting a moment, then turning to Drowning Bear.*)

Don't you think it would be better if they all went to the West?

DROWNING BEAR

Why should they go to the West, Mr. President? That changes nothing.

(*Harrison looks at Webster, then glances down.*)

HARRISON

I begin to see what you mean.

DROWNING BEAR

Mr. President, Drowning Bear is an old man. He can remember his father telling how he fought at Yorktown with General Washington. First the white man came over the Blue Ridge and built cabins in the coves of the mountains, then he spread out all the way to the Mississippi.

The march of the white man is toward the West, and some day he will take everything between the two oceans. It is foolish to believe he will not trouble the Indians in the western territory! The white man's nature is not like that. Sooner or later he will cover the whole continent!

HARRISON

What do you think the answer is?

DROWNING BEAR

The Indian will never be safe until he is part of the government, like the white man himself. Perhaps the government means to act in good faith, but individual men lie, and cheat, and steal, both the Indians and the whites. The only answer is to make the Cherokee—all Indians—American citizens!

HARRISON

Suppose we find it impossible to do that?

DROWNING BEAR

(*Shifting on his cane.*)

The day of the Red Man is passing. Sequoyah knew it thirty years ago. Junaluska told us that before he went to the West. Now Drowning Bear can see it too. All we ask is to stay in North Carolina, those who are left. Most of the people are good to us. We are never bothered by the state government. We take the steep hillsides and tend them with our hands—and let the white man keep the fertile valleys.

(*Harrison sits for a moment with his head bowed, then he takes his shoes and slips them on, straightens, rises slowly.*)

HARRISON

Thirty years ago, just before the Battle of Tippecanoe, I tried to tell Tecumseh and his crazy brother the same thing you have just said, but they wouldn't listen, so I had to go in and clean them out. I tried to tell Andy Jackson, but he wouldn't listen either. Now you come to me with the same proposition, thirty years too late.

WEBSTER

(*Pleading.*)
Too late?

HARRISON

The seeds of hate have been planted, and the weeds are still growing. It will take many years to change all that.
(*Turning to Drowning Bear with a smile.*)
But we can try! Democratic government means nothing as long as races continue to hate each other! I want the Indians to become citizens, and the Negroes too—but I can't just wave my hand and have it happen. I can promise you one thing—as long as I'm in the White House, the government will not bother you. You get North Carolina to protect you against the white trash that causes all the trouble. I think North Carolina can handle it! I'll send a letter to the governor—and I'll send a copy to that Major Davis you mentioned.
(*Offering Drowning Bear his hand.*)
And the federal government will stand behind you!
(*Drowning Bear drops his cane and seizes the hand of Harrison.*)

WEBSTER

(*Almost overcome.*)
Mr. President!
(*The lights go down and the music is a strange, restless theme that merges into "Mine Eyes Have Seen the Glory."*)

SCENE 5

NARRATOR

Two weeks later, before he could even select all his cabinet, William Henry Harrison was dead.
Up and down inland rivers, across southern cotton fields, down the rainy streets of northern industrial towns, vast shadows were gathering, and it would be many years before anyone would find time to pay much attention to the Cherokee. War was coming—times were changing—

America was growing up—the past was becoming a hazy dream.

But in the Great Smokies time flowed on. Drowning Bear was right when he told the President that he was an old man, old and very lonely. But he had found peace, because at last Sequoyah's dream was coming true. His people were the friends of their white neighbors.

> *(The lights come up on the center stage; the music changes to an old-fashioned dance tune; and a crowd of gaily-costumed pioneers, both white and Indian, fills the area with a colorful dance as the people whirl and courtsey, talking and laughing. The dance is in full swing as Drowning Bear and Will Thomas come in to watch, smiling and chatting. Drowning Bear is very gray, stooped, and leaning heavily on his cane. The dance is in full swing when the door of the house up right opens and Mrs. Perkins comes out waving her arms for quiet.)*

MRS. PERKINS

Quiet—quiet—stop it!

> *(The music stops and the people stand puzzled. Mrs. Perkins continues, hands on hips.)*

Well!

LEADER

Aw, Miz Perkins, we're jist celebratin' the new baby—when it comes!

MRS. PERKINS

What's got into you hellions? How do you expect Nundayeli to have a baby with all this racket goin' on? Git out yonder under that clump o' trees and dance. We got to have quiet aroun' here! Go on—git!

> *(She shoos them out at left and they go laughing and joking. Suyeta, one of the dancers, crosses his arms and refuses to move.)*

You too!

SUYETA

I'm the father! I'm going to stay right here!

MRS. PERKINS
(*Pushing him across toward the bench up right where Drowning Bear and Will Thomas are seated.*)
Well, git over there with Drownin' Bear, where I can git you if I need you. The rest o' you'ns clear out o' here!
(*The dancers go, and Mrs. Perkins retreats into the house up right. Drowning Bear turns to Thomas.*)

DROWNING BEAR
Drowning Bear never saw this much trouble over one baby!

THOMAS
(*Laughing.*)
What's wrong with you?—about to become a grandfather, and you sit here calm as a cucumber!

DROWNING BEAR
Suyeta spoils his wife! You watch—next time she'll want a doctor!
(*Thomas is laughing as Major Davis, in civilian clothes, comes in quickly from the left. Thomas sees him and gets up quickly to meet him with a handshake.*)

THOMAS
Major Davis! Welcome to the village! Glad to see you! Look, Drowning Bear, here's the U. S. District Attorney!

DROWNING BEAR
(*Getting up slowly with a deep sigh.*)
More trouble! What have we done now?

DAVIS
(*Smiling as he shakes hands with Drowning Bear.*)
Nothing yet—but I've got my eye on you.

THOMAS
Sit down and rest. You're just in time for dinner.

DAVIS
I can't stop now. I've just come from Raleigh—I still have a long ride back to Cherokee County.

(*Taking out some papers and handing them to Thomas.*)
I brought you the deed on that property—the rest of that piece down at Birdtown—all registered in good order.

Thomas
(*Glancing through the papers.*)
That's good. The way they come drifting back from Oklahoma, we need all the land we can get.

Drowning Bear
(*Turning away.*)
Drowning Bear is afraid! Some day they will take back the land!

Davis
I don't think so. We've worked out a pretty good case in the last few years. I believe we can hold what we have. Some day we'll have a reservation here, then no one can touch you.

Thomas
(*Holding up the papers in amazement.*)
Major Davis, there must be some mistake here. This deed calls for that whole section, all the way from the river back to the top of the mountain. That's a hundred acres more than we asked for—I gave you only four hundred dollars—

Davis
(*Pulling on his gloves.*)
Well—let's say the rest is a birthday present for Suyeta's boy. Has he come yet?

Suyeta
Any time now!

Thomas
(*His hand on Davis' shoulder.*)
You put up a hundred dollars yourself.

Davis
(*Ignoring Thomas' remark.*)
Keep that old man out of trouble.

DROWNING BEAR

Drowning Bear is busy keeping everybody else out of trouble.

> (*Davis smiles and as the two men look at each other, Drowning Bear comes to him and shakes his hand, then he turns and goes slowly back to his seat, sits down, rests his chin on his cane, and gazes at the ground. Davis goes out quickly. Thomas pockets the papers, glances at Drowning Bear.*)

THOMAS

What are you thinking about?

DROWNING BEAR

Something Sequoyah said many years ago.

SUYETA

(*Peering suddenly off right.*)
Look! Another one is coming back!

THOMAS

(*Going off toward the left.*)
Well! I'll go call the others!
> (*Suyeta is peering anxiously at right.*)

SUYETA

Looks like he walked all the way from Oklahoma. That makes five this month!
> (*The door of the house opens and Mrs. Perkins leans out with a broad smile.*)

MRS. PERKINS

Suyeta—come in here!

SUYETA

(*Running toward the house.*)
Already?
> (*He disappears inside. Drowning Bear rises slowly and peers toward the newcomer at right. Junaluska enters, a gray old man with a cane. Drowning Bear peers again, suddenly lifts his hands and starts toward Junaluska.*)

DROWNING BEAR
(*Deeply affected.*)
Junaluska!
(*He drops his cane and embraces the other.*)
Junaluska has come home!
(*The villagers, led by Thomas, hurry in from the left. Drowning Bear turns to the villagers.*)
Little Will! Look who's here!
(*The people gather excitedly around Junaluska.*)

THOMAS
(*Seizing his hand.*)
Welcome home, Junaluska! Welcome home!

JUNALUSKA
(*A little nervous.*)
Junaluska will not trouble his old friends. He has only a little time to live. There is a good hiding place on Deep Creek. Junaluska will go there.

THOMAS
You'll stay right here in the village! We'll take care of you!

WHITE MAN
You need somethin' to eat, an' a long rest. You come to my house!

JUNALUSKA
No! That would make trouble with the other white men! Junaluska only came back to see his people once more. He has heard nothing since he left. Junaluska could not forget the twilight mist in the beech trees—he remembered the evening wind speaking through the pines and high valleys. He remembered the mighty words of Sequoyah—he kept seeing the face of Sam Houston—he remembered how Tsali stood up to die so that our people might live—

THOMAS
Times have changed, Junaluska. You can live right here in the village. All the people are your friends.

DROWNING BEAR

Will Thomas will give you some new shoes to pinch your feet, and some new clothes—and he will find you a piece of land down along the river. The farmers will give you grain. Junaluska will have a house and a piece of land!

JUNALUSKA

(*Bewildered.*)

Junaluska does not understand.

THOMAS

Never mind. You're home now!

WHITE MAN

Come with me an' get some food in you. Then you can rest.

JUNALUSKA

My people are happy?

THOMAS

(*Indicating the smiling crowd.*)

Just look at them!

(*The door of the house up right bursts open and Suyeta comes running out.*)

SUYETA

It's a son! It's a son!

(*There is a great murmur of excitement as the people rush to congratulate Suyeta.*)

THOMAS

(*Hurrying to Drowning Bear to shake his hand.*)

You hear? Nundayeli has a baby! Drowning Bear is a grandfather!

(*The music begins softly in the background.*)

DROWNING BEAR

(*Smiling and nodding.*)

Drowning Bear is glad. This makes him very happy. You hear, Junaluska?

JUNALUSKA

(*With a tired smile.*)

Now Tsali has a grandchild. Tsali's grandchild will someday be an American citizen. Now Tsali lives again!
(Nodding and smiling.)
Winter dies—spring comes. It is good!
(The people are crowding around Suyeta, and Will Thomas is congratulating Drowning Bear once more, as Junaluska turns slowly and begins hobbling toward the right on his cane. The choir is humming in the background as the Narrator speaks.)

NARRATOR

In the beginning was the land. In the beginning was freedom. In the beginning was peace.
(As the Narrator and the music continue, Drowning Bear and Will Thomas notice Junaluska and start after him. Drowning Bear restrains him down right, but Junaluska shakes his head and hobbles slowly on, one hand on his heart.)
Once upon a time, out of the darkness of tragedy, a man said, "I will lift up mine eyes unto the hills . . . ."
(Junaluska is moving toward the valley at the right. A beam of light falls on his departing figure, and the lights on the center stage diminish. Drowning Bear takes another step toward Junaluska and holds out his hand, while Will Thomas stands near by. The crowd has moved slowly to the center.)
Once upon a time, out of the darkness of tragedy, a race of people looked beyond the years and devoted itself to the dream of its great leader, when he said, "It is not that a man's skin is black, or red, or white. Choose the way of peace. Take all men as your brothers."
(Junaluska is disappearing from sight; Drowning Bear stands with one hand held out toward him; Thomas has one hand on Drowning Bear's shoulder. The choir is singing at full volume. The stage lights give way to a broad green flood of light that covers the mountainside back of the stages.)
This, then, was the dream of the Cherokee.
This, then, is America!

Unto These Hills was first presented the summer of 1950, July 1 through September 4, at the Mountainside Theatre, Cherokee, North Carolina. The staff for the opening season of this production was as follows:

Directed by Harry Davis
Settings and technical direction by Lynn Gault
Choreography by Foster Fitz-Simons
Music by Jack Frederick Kilpatrick
Lighting by James Riley
Costumes by Suzanne Davis
Music direction by Anne Martin
Properties by George McKinney
At the organ, Will Headlee
Promotion director, E. Carl Sink
General manager, Carol White

The Cherokee Historical Association is a non-profit, chartered corporation sponsored by the Western North Carolina Associated Communities, with the purpose of perpetuating the history and traditions of the Cherokee Indians. The officers of The Cherokee Historical Association are:

Harry E. Buchanan, *Chairman*
Percy B. Ferebee, *Vice-Chairman*
Joe Jennings, *Treasurer*
Molly Arneach, *Secretary*

www.ingramcontent.com/pod-product-compliance
Lightning Source LLC
Chambersburg PA
CBHW030118010526
44116CB00005B/297